Table of Contents

Nicole Newman is an inspiring motivational writer, public speaker and business networker. She was born in Washington DC and grew up in the City of Brotherly Love, Philadelphia. A product of Julia R. Reynolds Masterman School and the High School of Engineering and Science, she was gifted enough to acquire a strong work ethic. Though an altercation in 1989 left her with a stab wounds to the face, neck and right arm she was honored with the most improved student award upon graduation.

She started her college career at the University of North Carolina at Greensboro. In her second year she was involved in a car accident that left her with a broken femur bone and a sublegal hematoma to the brain. Although she was unable to complete school at the University of NC at Greensboro, 2 months later while on crutches she transferred to Temple University and graduate magna cum laud from the Fox school of

Business with a Bachelors of Business Administration in Risk Management and Insurance, Management Information Systems and a minor in Human Resources. She went on to complete her MBA at the prestigious Robert H. Smith school of Business at the University of Maryland majoring in Finance.

Nicole started her professional Information Technology career at CIGNA where she found a niche in database design and reporting. She was fascinated by putting data in a sequence that buildd information. After a 15 year run, she ended her corporate career at the global consulting firm of Deloitte Touche Tomatsu. She left to pursue her passion in entrepreneurialism and bridging the digital divide.

Nicole started her company, Newman Networks in April of 2006 which owned www.diversephilly.com, a website for businesses to share the costs of advertising. In just the second year, the company quadrupled revenue. With over 2000 LinkedIn connections, 6000 Facebook friends and 80 testimonials, the company made a massive network in the local marketplace. This is just one of the testimonials – "Nicole Newman is an outstanding individual. She is an incredible connector and exemplifies in her daily life the proof that networking is the key to building a successful business. Nicole cares most about her clients, colleagues and friends; assisting them in building strong relationships that will lead to company growth and success. Anyone doing business in the Greater Philadelphia region should get to know Nicole immediately. She will absolutely take your business to the next level." said Kate Bay, regional account executive Greater Philadelphia Chamber of Commerce.

FOREWORD

How do I begin? How do I journal my purpose?

The year 2009 started out with a bang! The seeds of the entrepreneurial forest the Creator planted on my heart in 2006 were beginning to bear fruit! Accomplishing the goal is so close I can feel and touch it. The wealth and abundance is so close, I can taste it. BUT as the remembrance of God is the center of my entire world, and on this journey it is up to Him, and He willed that I STOP.

I feel compelled to relive and journal all the sadness and pain before.

So, how do I begin, how do I begin without breaking down and crying…. How do I open up the book to let you know, my pain is the pain of my children, my parents, my culture, my country and my nation? My pain goes back generations and generations before I was born. As the Creator has shown me many times, It is as if it were said to me, "Your pain and sadness was brought on so you could LOVE deeply; see the depth of your pain is the depth of your LOVE.

The depth of my pain from being a shy, overweight teenager with very low self-esteem is still there; from being teased about my hair (before locks were in style) or the way I dressed (not much selection for a 12 year old child who wears a size 20) is still there. The depth of my pain from being stabbed in the face, neck and arms (just missing my jugular vein) with a butcher knife on the 15th street platform at 3:30 in the afternoon by my ex-best friend is still there; from having a father who has never said he loved me; from breaking my femur bone in a car accident while on my way back to college and having to sit out a semester and transfer to my Temple University from the University of North Carolina at Greensboro is still there... And the depth of my pain from being single; an unmarried woman, who on the clutches of experiencing the phenomenon of birth, gets the cruel blow of an 8-month still born child on what was supposed to be a beautiful day for a baby shower. That pain caused 350 days of depression which shut down my reproductive system. Shawn Aaron Newman, you will forever be in my heart.

Now I have to make room to add the depth of my children's pain from having a father who decides to walk away and torture his three children my mailing them Christmas presents on January 18th, 2009 (without a note or a phone call!)

But I am strong. I am a woman; a woman born of another woman who is born of another woman born of another. I hold the strength of my grandmother, Ms. Marion Payne, who at 16 got married and started a family with four children by the age of 23. Her husband strayed from the family path and my grandmother decided to leave. This was unheard of in 1943. She had to survive away from her family with four children in tow, and survive she did. She had hard choices to make. The family was split apart, but it was her through her strength and God's will that she made it and she never gave up. When she found husband number two, she was taking care of a housebound woman and her family once again reunited. My grandmother and her second husband had five more children together, with my mom being the baby girl.

At my mom's tender age of four, her father (my grandfather) passed away. He was on a fishing trip when the boat capsized and drowned my grandfather in the river. It was up to my grandmother once again to hold the family together. Unfortunately, in 1970, the house caught fire from wiring in the basement, killing the housebound woman, my five baby cousins from Aunt Tammy (not her real name) - ages eight years old to three months old and my two pre-teen cousin's ages eight and ten from Aunt Linda (not her real name) and once again, the family was torn apart. My mom was lucky. She was taken in by her BFF's (BFF is best friend forever) family for almost a year while she was attending high school.

And my grandmother's strength was passed to my mom, who got married to my father and decided to leave (do you hear the broken record?) because he strayed from the family path. She had hard choices to make, like moving into my father's parents' house and working her way up in Corporate America and once again, moving in with her BFF.

But I refuse to let this be a book about dysfunction in the African American community. I refuse to be another statistic about the dismal cycle of poverty brought on by another broken home, or to be a statistic about the number of highly educated women who are still single because the pool of African–

American men who are not incarcerated is increasingly shrinking. I refuse to let my sons grow up in a world where they only have two tracks – the low-paying mail room or incarceration. I have been gifted with the awesome responsibility of loving you. I have been gifted with the awesome responsibility of showing you how to dream again and wake up to the dawn of a new era. Barack Obama is the president! Wake up people this is a new world!

The path to wealth and abundance is full of potholes, but as I have witnessed, it was that pain of a still born child that brought three beautiful, intelligent children into my world. It was the pain of Martin Luther King Jr. getting shot on the balcony that allowed Barack Obama to be president. It was the pain of having my children's father walk away that will allow me to live as the QUEEN I know I am. It was the pain of the twenty-something years of low self-esteem that allowed me to have focus and determination and not give a DAMN about what someone thinks about me! See, the depth of my pain is the depth of my LOVE.

This book is meant to inspire you to accept you. And only when you accept you and heal yourself will we be able to walk together and seek the blessings of this world.

This is how we begin...

We are suffering...Confucius said "The father who does not teach his son his duties is equally as guilty with the son who neglects them." That is the price paid for being daddy's little girl.

Chapter 1

This will begin at the center of my heart: My dad. My dad is the reason for my existence. It is his behavior that drives me to love. I am in love with Love. I actually grew up with a guy named Love, and was just so in love with his name. It is because my dad never loved me that I act the way that I do. I guess I was in my late 20's at a therapy session, which is conversing with my mom, that I began to understand my Dad's behavior. He can never love me because he doesn't love himself.

My dad and my mom are from two opposite worlds. My dad's family, the Newman's, were originally farmers with lots of land in Virginia. My grandfather owned a landscaping company and my grandparents bought land and used sweat equity to build a home out in the well to-do area of the main line. This was where we would drive by mansions to get to their house in Lower Merion, Pennsylvania. When I was growing up, the house seemed to me like paradise. They lived life in a big house in the suburbs with a circular driveway and lots of space. They had a picture perfect family: Mom the homemaker, Dad the entrepreneur, three sons, a baby girl, and the dog. My dad grew up getting material possessions from his parents, but he never got what he really needed; love.

My Mom grew up in the inner city of Washington, D.C., daughter of a widowed mom with nine children. Her family was deeded their house by a lady my grandmother befriended. She did not have a picture perfect family. My grandmother was a cleaning lady who worked for the government. My mom hardly ever saw my grandmother and there was never enough money or things for everybody. But my mom got what every child needs: lots of Love. She had love from her mom, her sisters, her brothers, and the various other children my grandmother raised at any given time. It still takes a village to raise a child. See, my mom was smart - incredibly smart, and a writer too! She met my dad because she was awarded a full scholarship to attend prestigious Bryn Mawr College out on the Main Line.

Though I cannot verify these details , I know my mom must have been a shock to my Dad's system. He attended Conestoga High School where he was with but a handful of black students. Most of his girlfriends were Caucasian. My grandmother, who is very fair, was raised with the mindset of "white is right". Though there were only a handful of black students at Bryn Mawr College, my mom stood out. My mom, at the time, had a very attractive bush, she had dated all black men, and was raised with the mindset of "I'm black and proud". My Dad is fairly light and my mom is fairly dark. I guess, it is true, opposites do attract!

So, in my mom's sophomore year, after nine months of a great labor, at 8 a.m. on Thursday, January 4th, 1973, Nicole Michelle Newman was born. My dad was back in Philadelphia when I came out of my mother's womb without the doctor's assistance. Even then I was head strong!

My mom and dad tried to do the right thing and in Mid-August of 1973, they got married. It was the shortest marriage I'd ever heard of (next to the Hollywood marriages that last just days) after seven months of trying, my mom gave up. My dad neglected me so badly that she left to protect what little self-esteem I had left. My dad worked two jobs to support his family, so I would be excited to see him finally come home, and he would walk right by me like I wasn't even there. I would talk to him with my goo-goo and gaa–gaa and want to sit and play with him and he would ignore me like I was in the way of his life. These repressed feelings still haunt me today, and I have a huge soft spot for fathers who are taking care of their daughters.

My mom says my father lives physically, but his mind and spirit are gone. I did not understand at the time, but now realize my father is but a shell; the body is there, but the mind can no longer think because the spirit is dead.

How? How does this happen to a man who is 6'1" inches tall and 260 pounds? How does this happen to a man I saw maneuver a two ton flat-bed tractor trailer with a paver on it up a winding embankment to get the job done? How does this happen to a man who could fix a car, landscape your driveway and drive an 18 wheeler across the country all at the same time; a father that should be the center of a little girl's universe? A father's love will be the measure of any man that enters that girl's life. A father's love will determine how men view her as confident, self-assured and worthy of a good man - or insecure, vulnerable and unworthy of any man. His spirit left because of his parents. They (mainly my grandmother) denied their children of an essential building block of life, the gift of Love.

The big house on the main line, even though it was pretty on the outside, was full of tension on the inside. Whenever my grandmother stepped in the room, she brought deceit and mistrust with her; some people have positive energy and attract kind words in the room, and some people bring negative energy to an environment. Even though she is over 80 years-old now, I recently saw her at a funeral, and she was at it again, sitting with one of her sisters gossiping about someone at the funeral, making snide remarks and faces. You would think that they would have learned by now. I'll tell you a story my mom told me:

My mom dated my dad while she was in college, and naturally since my grandmother was a homemaker she could cook very well. Every chance my mom would get, she tried to stay in my grandmother's kitchen. Sunday dinner of course was the big meal of the week, and the whole family would be around the table. One Sunday, when my mom was dating my dad before I was born, the family - my grandmother, grandfather, dad, two uncles, aunt Joan, and my mom, were eating dinner, and the table was very still. It was quiet because the tension in the air was so thick. My grandmother looked my Aunt Joan, who was just 11 years old at the time and said to her words a mother should not say to any child, "I wish you were never born…". My aunt sat at the table and cried. My dad, who was 19, his younger brother Kenny, who was 15, and my uncle Robert, who was 22, said nothing, and continued to eat dinner while my aunt cried so much that her eyes turned red. There was no love in that house.

My mom had a lot of courage to do what she did after she left my dad. For a time, we lived in my grandmother's big house. We were a part of the family now, and my dad would still ignore me. My mom did not finish school, so the jobs she had did not bring in enough money for us to live on our own. However, as soon as she could, we moved our belongings into a one-bedroom apartment in Philadelphia…

Chapter 2: Gigi

My daughter, Sahar, and my mom, have a special bond. Since the day Sahar was born, she has been my mom's child. Unlike me, Sahar is shy and quiet by nature. She likes to please everybody, she is non-confrontational and wants to be an only child. Every four weeks or so she asks me can she go to Grandma's house. My mom loves my daughter Sahar to death. She says, "Grandchildren are the gift for not strangling your children!" Mom, I know we had some rough patches like my teenager years from ages 12-17 that drove you crazy, but I promise I am better now. I will tell more about that in chapter five. I used to be a little jealous of their closeness, but now I see where it comes from.

My grandmother, affectionately known as Gigi, when my children were born, meant the world to me. Even though she passed away at the young age of 89 in 2004, she was the original "Phenomenal Woman!" Gigi was all of that, and a bag of chips! I admired her strength and her conviction. My grandmother was the "Soul Food" image of family. She had the big house that was full of laughter. Yes, we laughed a lot in that house to hide the pain, and yes, she raised me and three of my cousins to give our parents a break, and yes, she went to church every Sunday without fail. She was on the trustee board, president of the pastor's aid club, member of the flower ministry, charity board, funeral committee and any other position, except the minister at Greater New Hope Baptist Church for over 50 years! I know we don't like to talk about this much but she was also a Tither! (told you she was all that!)

My grandmother had a 1,000 watt smile and loved everyone who had the pleasure of knowing her. She was wealthy beyond her modest income. I did not learn her journey for a long time but from the conversations with the family, she lived an extraordinary life. My grandmother was born and raised right here in South Philadelphia. Even though she got married and moved off to Washington D.C. to be with her husband, that South Philadelphia toughness was engraved in her from the beginning. She was born Marion Burrell on July 16, 1914, seventh child of the family. There were six older brothers, then my grandma, then Aunt Berthea and then Aunt Ida.

At the young age of 16, my grandmother got married and shortly thereafter started a family. As her husband started to stray, my grandmother said enough is enough. Even though my grandfather was financially taking care of the family, my grandmother's integrity would not allow her to stay. She knew that if she accepted a man who cheated, he would continue to cheat (great lesson!), so she had to put her foot down and go. She would not settle for money, she sought happiness. As a single mom with four children, she struggled and was forced to let her children live with strangers while she worked to find a way to make it on her own. Her oldest daughter, Edith, even went away to boarding school. It was at boarding school on June 6th, that she got sick with appendicitis and died on the operating table at the young age of 16. It seems that losing our children is the family curse. There is no pain greater than losing a child, and even through that pain, my grandmother's spirit carried on.

My grandmother was blessed with Flossy Iverson. They had been best friends (BFF's) for years. Flossy did not have much family, so my grandmother and her children were like her own family. Flossy wound up getting sick and becoming home-bound, so my grandmother stepped in to take care of her. Flossy's house was in the Petworth neighborhood of Washington, D.C., not far from Howard University. She lived in the twin house. It was the only house on the block with a driveway. Technically, the house was four bedrooms and one and ½ bathrooms, but to my grandma's family, every room could be a bedroom. At one time, over 20 people lived in the house. There were people sleeping in the basement and my uncle lived in the attic for over 30 years! Like I said, Grandma has the big house just like the movie, Soul Food! My grandmother eventually moved all of her children in, and once again, the family was reunited.

She also found love again with her second husband, my grandfather, James D. Payne. Shortly after they got married, he was shipped off to fight in World War II. As soon as he returned, baby booming season begun, and out came Aunt Linda, Aunt Tammy, Uncle Bobby, My mom, and my Uncle Joe. Unfortunately, at the tender age of four, my grandfather was removed from my mom's life. Tragically, he was killed in a capsized boat on a fishing trip. Once again, my grandmother had to find strength to live through another death in the family.

My mom says growing up was a mad house. She, like my daughter Sahar, is shy and quiet by nature. Their favorite activity is reading books. My mom spent a lot of time in the only room that gave her peace: the bathroom. That was the only place she could be alone. My grandma found joy in serving others. Because she had lived through all the tragedies and was able to keep her family together, she would do just about anything for anybody. Some people, unfortunately, took advantage of this, but it never stopped my grandmother from continuing to give.

During the late 1960's to the early 1980's, my family was affected by drugs flowing into the black, urban communities. We had numerous uncles and friends come to our house and steal everything from the china to money straight out of my grandmother's purse. The climax happened on Thanksgiving Day, 1970. This is my understanding from the stories that have been passed down:

My uncle and his friends were getting high in the basement. They plugged a heater to warm up the basement in an old outlet. The heater started an electrical fire that went through the walls. Mostly everyone got out except the children that were trapped upstairs and my grandma's housebound BFF, Aunt Flossy. My Aunt Linda's children, ages eight and ten perished. Aunt Flossy and my Aunt Tammy's five children, ages two months to nine years, also died. My grandmother was not even home at the time. Even though she was not there, she felt as though she let the family down; she lost her BFF and seven of her grandchildren. You would never know from the outside that her heart was broken, because she, like me, looked at life as a glass half-full instead of a glass half-empty.

Growing up, that warm spirit was the glue that bonded me to my grandmother. She passed away when my daughter was just three years old, and Sahar fondly remembers her to this day. By the time Sahar was born, my grandmother had a pacemaker and was blind from a stroke. But she would still be drawn like the rest of us to my grandmother's spirit. Every chance we got, my mom and I would catch Amtrak down to D.C. We would take the trip almost every year for Labor Day, Thanksgiving, Christmas, Easter, Memorial Day, and the fourth of July. Even though my grandma had a big house, my mom and I would sleep in my grandmother's bed. I remember that on a couple of occasions my grandmother gave up her bed and slept on a chair to make sure we were comfortable. Now I understand why my grandmother had such a warm spirit. It is the pain that lets us understand and appreciate Love.

My grandmother had 18 grandchildren, but I knew that I was her favorite. Even in the rough middle school years, my grandmother protected me like a hawk. I had the privilege of spending every summer in D.C. from the 6th to the 9th grade, and she would not let me go anywhere. At the time, I thought she was being mean, but now I understand that she would not be able to live if something happened to me. She had seen death one time too many. My cousins, Russell and Joe, whom she was raising at the time, could do anything, but not me. I really didn't complain I just basked in the glow of her love. These are my thoughts about my ever-present role model, Mrs. Marion Payne:

Even though you are no longer present here on earth, you are present in me. I am fulfilling the path that you trail blazed for me. You have laid a foundation of wisdom in me to know who I am. Success is not material wealth, success is living a lifetime of caring and sharing. Success is loving people and being a blessing to others. My success is raising children to carry on the spirit that you have given me, I have been fortunate, like you, to have five BFF's who benefit me so I can benefit others. Even though people will use and abuse, I will stay true to the giving spirit that you laid upon me: loving others is the honor I give to you. Thank you grandma, for allowing your pain, like my own, to be the spirit that allows us to love.

They say…. "You become like the 5 people you spend the most time with."
CHOOSE CAREFULLY

Chapter 3: My BFF's

They say "It takes a village to raise a child." My friends have stayed friends for over 25 years. Like my grandmother, I am attached to my BFF's. We raise our children in a village. TEAM work makes the DREAM work. Tiffany, Myesha, Ayana, Latifa and Kina, those are my BFF's. A lot of people wondered how I got so much done as a single mom of a then seven, five and four year old. Yes, I run a network marketing company, a traditional business, and a household, as a single mom, and unfortunately, a substitute dad. My neighbors always give me props for Father's Day! I am able to get it all done because I am WE. We, me and the crew (my BFF's) work in harmony to raise our children in the village. We are a group of like-minded individuals who respect each other's differences and value our friendship. We have learned each other's quirks over the last 25 years. I know I have many, but we communicate well enough to work out our differences. Each one of my friends has stopped speaking to me for a year or more, but we are bonded like glue. 25 years will put your friendships to the test, and that is why they have become my Best Friends Forever.

My BFF's believe in me. They have given their time, money and effort to make sure Nicole Newman gets it done. It is their belief in me that continues to drive me on the bad days, like the days when I hear that a client did not pay (accounts payable is a real pain), or the days when I found out my prospect is going with another company, or when I feel like it everything is just too much. It is their belief that gets me out of the blues to strengthen me.

Whenever I am out and about, the village is taking care of the family. For me to do anything, careful coordination must be achieved. My children were enrolled in three different schools (I spend two hours a day shuffling them around), but one of my BFF's will step up to the plate and make sure they are taken care of. The village my BFF's developed allows me to show love to my customers while my children are in school, and while I am out networking Monday, Tuesday, Thursdays and Saturday night. The village is making sure my children are doing their homework, feeding them dinner, brushing their teeth, getting my children in bed and taking them to school in the morning, so I can make the environment of success once a month for the DiversePhilly networking event at 7:30 in the morning. I REPRESENT the village. Nas, I got mad love for you: I honored you by giving my son your name. My family says things like, "You are all your children have." I DON'T THINK SO. It takes a village to raise a child. My children will not be limited by my weaknesses; they will find strength in others. Yes, I am a mom, but I have no patience for homework . Where I am weak, they are strong.

When I was given this awesome responsibility, I remember saying I can't do this by myself. So He brought into my life the people who made it happen. My BFF's were planted years ago to go on this journey with me. Unbeknownst to me, when I said yes, they also said yes. My BFF's have entrusted me to lift my community and change all of our tax brackets. They have entrusted me to build the relationships necessary to show the world that we can love ourselves and grow together. They have believed in my ability to do this even when I was borrowing money from them! I am WE and I represent the village.

How does one find so much love between five friends? How does one find the bonds that last a lifetime? What my friends have taught me s that I had to be a friend to find a friend. Growing up as an only child, I was not in an environment to learn how to be a friend. When we moved to 61st and Walnut Street in 1983, I would come home from school and sit in my mom's window from 3:30 to 6 PM and watch the neighborhood children play outside. I sat and watched them play for over a year. I was too afraid to come outside and play with them. In my mind, I thought they were wild, but really, I was afraid of being rejected.

Tiffany with all her innocence and caring actually met my mom first as my mom was coming home from work. My mom introduced BFF #1 to me in 1984. Within a few days, Tiff was over my house and she introduced me to rapper-supastar, Myesha, BFF #2. Even then, at her young age of 9, she was destined to be a supastar. She was already studying acting at Freedom Theatre and had an uncanny ability of knowing what to say to get her way. My Mom had a sneaky suspicion that she was "bad", and my mom was right. I got in lots of trouble hanging out with her. But I also had a rocking good time with that trouble maker. When Myesha, Tiff and I got together, we just knew we were Salt-N-Pepa! Myesha was Salt, Tiffany was Pepa, and I was Spinderella. I used to wake up every day to a Lady B tape I made from her show on Sundays (12-5 pm for all the old-heads reading this). My favorite song was "I'll Take Your Man" (O, the irony)- and I just had a flashback moment. Okay, back to the BFF's...

Myesha, Tiffany and I were instant bonds. We were female 'only-children' so we had a bond that went beyond the superficial. We were able to identify and see each other's pain without using our voices to communicate. Usually, in groups of three, two people team up and turn against the third, but in our case that rarely happened. The very first time we got together, Tiffany and Myesha started arguing over my paper collection. I had given Tiffany some of my paper and Myesha was trying to take the paper I had given to Tiffany. So I delegated that they each got an equal portion of the paper, and then our roles were set. My role was to get all of us on the same page. I have the same role today, just with different people. And I still love paper to this day.

Tiffany and Myesha actually introduced me to BFF's numbers #3 and #4, the sisters Ayana and Latifa. Ayana and Latifa were a lot different than us. They were being raised in a home with a mom and a dad (what a shock!), and they were Muslim girls. I developed much respect for the Muslim Religion by just seeing how my BFF's were raised. They could not go across the street to Myesha's house, but luckily for me, they lived two houses away. Ayana was the older one – she was the mom to us, even at the young age of 11, but Latifa, who was only seven years old, was the wild child. A lot of people think I am head strong, but this little girl cursed me out!

In front of my house we used to have rock columns. One day, I leaned on the rock column and it collapsed. Everyone was laughing and I got mad and blamed it on Latifa. Even though she was half my size and four years younger, she was not intimated, and cursed me out in front of the whole crew. At the end of the day, the crew stopped laughing at me and began to appreciate her. I thank her for that, because she made everyone stop laughing at me, which is all I really wanted.

Latifa and Ayana were raised in a different culture. They were my first two clients on DiversePhilly. Their family raised them to make jobs, not to work for other people. Tiffany and Myesha both worked for Latifa and Ayana at one time. I am taking their model and grooming my children to own businesses. Their mom was a school teacher, and even then I knew when I became a mom, this family would be instrumental in my family's success. Latifa and Ayana have an older sister who I continue to look up to.

Their older sister, Sahar, is the black version of Grace Kelly. When she walks, she walks like royalty. She expected men to do certain things; I never saw her open a car door, she was to be chauffeured. I admired that in her, and she was the first person I knew that went off to college. I remember thinking that if I ever had a child I would name her Sahar, and as that was planted in my mind, when my daughter came out I honored Sahar by giving my daughter her name.

BFF #5 is the only one that did not grow up on 61st and Walnut Street. Kina, is a friend from high school. Whenever I made a new friend, they would be introduced to the Walnut Street crew and evaluated.

None of my so called friends (I must have introduced at least 20) made it through the evaluation from the crew. My friends could tell when someone was being nice to me just to get something. I was and still am a giant, soft, cuddly teddy bear that just has a rough exterior. We are very protective of each other. BFF#5 made it through because she is just a good person. She has her own set of quirks, but we all have them, and how we communicate is the make or break factor.

I met BFF #5 in the 9th grade; high school. I guess in the middle of the year, I lent her a text book, and when she went to return the book to me she put it on top of my locker. Needless to say, I never got the book. In the 10th grade, the school would not give me any books until I had paid for the lost text book. I confronted my friend but she said she was not paying for it. At this time, I was about 220 pounds, 5'10" tall. My friend is 5' 4" tall about 120 pounds. I knew I could take her. By the end of the day, the whole school knew we were going to have the show down. On the way home, the fight was on. I hit her once and remember nothing else. She beat me up front of Temple University's McGonigle Hall.

As always, I look at the bright side of things. Her mom, who is now my second mom - I used to celebrate certain holidays with their family- came to the school the next day and paid for the book. In the 11th grade, Kina and I started getting close (It took me a year to get over the fact that she beat me up...). One day, I was over her house and she had a memorial wall with all the trophies she had won and the cut outs from being in the newspaper... I had fought a karate expert! I just looked at her while she cracked up... Kina, you got that! The moral of this story: don't judge a book by its cover. That is a lesson I use even to this day when I deal with the businesses in Newman Networks.

This is just an introduction to the key players in my life. Women understand that male friends and husbands come and go. The guy you are giving flowers to this year, you probably won't remember his name next year. If you are celebrating love year after year it is because you are celebrating a friend first! As my business partner told me, we cannot have anything else until we are friends first. A true friendship will go through some things, such as rough periods where you are fighting and mad at each, other but a true friendship will bring you back because you miss that person so much. A true friendship has a bond of love. I love my sister-girlfriends and I know without a shadow of a doubt that they love me. The dark days I went through, I did not go alone because my sister-girlfriends were right there. When I lost Shawn, two of my BFF's could be with me in a moment because they had experienced the loss of a child themselves. When I got stabbed on the platform at 15th street, I was the strength one of my BFF's needed when we also got stabbed four months later. When my house was being treated for lead paint four years ago, my family lived with one of my BFF's for a month! Those rough patches are the scars that bonded us together. It was the adversity and trials that make our friendship strong.

Now these bonds are being passed to our children. That is why we take pride in creating the village. I take this day to celebrate the love that allows me to live my dream every day. I celebrate you and cherish my five BFF's. God, thank you for allowing me to REPRESENT we. I thank you for giving my family sister-girlfriends. Even though I was born an only child, time has bonded me to five friends and I cannot

thank them enough for everything they do. I know I
have a mission to accomplish and you are the
compass that sets the path. Thank you for blessing me
with the tools and resources to build more
entrepreneurs and generate wealth in the village that
built me. My promise to you is to continue to do the
DARNED THING until that mission is accomplished.

"Don't you dare surround yourself with people who are not aware of the greatness that you are." Jo Blackwell-Preston

Chapter 4: Relationships

A lot of life is about relationships; relationships with our parents, with our children, with our BFFs, co-workers, spouses, and even with ourselves. Every relationship, good or bad, is a reflection of how we see ourselves. In business, the hardest part to grow a business is finding and recruiting talent. Personally, I look for hidden gems that can be bought low and trained to be sold high. First, talent is hard to find, especially if you are just looking at the surface (resume, connections, etc..), and second, you need high-quality with excellent communication skills to retain talent.

One of the best definitions of communication I have seen comes from the state of Washington public education system: "Communication is defined as a process by which we assign and convey meaning in an attempt to build shared understanding. This process requires a vast repertoire of skills in intrapersonal and interpersonal processing, listening, observing, speaking, questioning, analyzing, and evaluating. Use of these processes is developmental and transfers to all areas of life: home, school, community, work, and beyond." They say that 80% of all communication is non-verbal. Even though we spend most of our day communicating, texting is a barrier to the evaluation process that must occur to transfer the communication effectively.

The Wall Street Journal reported the findings of a survey of 480 companies that found that employers ranked communication abilities first among the desirable personal qualities of future employees (1998). In a report on fastest growing careers, the U.S. Department of Labor states that communication skills will be in demand across occupations well into the next century. In a national survey of 1,000 human resource managers, oral communication skills were identified as valuable for both obtaining employment and successful job performance.

I know my unique value in the marketplace is the ability to translate advances in technology into actionable results to increase profitability for business. Basically, I communicate well in business. Now my children, once again, are positioning me to transfer that skill set into a better balanced home life for them.

As an only child, I really did not have to learn communication skills. I basically had my needs fulfilled and knew what I needed to do to get my wants and desires fulfilled, i.e. get good grades and stay out of trouble. I broke that many times. It wasn't until the Deloitte experience at age 31 that I found out how my communication skills (or lack thereof) would impact my professional career. Understand that all cultures communicate differently:

I have observed that people of European descent like to talk in a sandwich; First comes the compliment, next comes the feedback then it ends with a compliment. This was very confusing to me. All I wanted to know was if I do a good job or not. I needed to put meaning behind the communication and it took too long to figure it out. African Americans like to shoot from the hip, we dish it straight so it can be received straight. Where I think that we as a people fail, is the follow-up communication. Just because we don't like an action, we are too easy to give up on the relationship.

That is why I read Relationships 101 by John C. Maxwell. A relationship is given depth by five factors -

RESPECT, Shared Experiences, TRUST, Reciprocity and Mutual Enjoyment.

1. Respect is to have positive esteem for a person by acting in a way that shows consideration for the other party involved. You can have no relationship with a person who is trying to "get over" on you or showing by their action no consideration for your well being. RESPECT is the essential building block to a relationship and unfortunately, the media, men- and even African-American Men- have shown that African-American women (as a group compared to others) deserve no respect by their actions of abandoning their children (About 80% of African American can expect to spend "a significant" portion of their childhood living without their biological fathers) and portraying women as hoes and b****es in videos, media outlets, etc. and allowing images of successful black men marrying and dating women outside of their race (when minorities marry outside their group, their spouses are usually white). Aretha Franklin's tune of R-E-S-P-E-C-T made in 1967 still holds true today. Without respect, there is

no relationship. Respect levels change over time. Most people get into a relationship with a certain respect level and the behaviors over time can gain or lose respect. This should be evaluated and communicated often.

2. Shared Experiences build reference points in our lives. This is where it is said that men are from Mars and women are from Venus. Most men have been taught to view sex as one-sided for their enjoyment where women have been taught sex is a shared experience. It took me too many years to figure this out and ladies, we must step up to the plate and warn, talk, and prepare our daughters for this reality. Sex should not be experienced until marriage, and marriage should be preceded by multiple other shared experiences that are mutually enjoyable to both parties involved (i.e. the five date rule).

3. TRUST is where you expose your vulnerabilities to people, hoping that they will not take advantage of your openness.

4. RECIPROCITY is a mutual or cooperative interchange of favors or privileges. I would

place TRUST AND RECIPROCITY in the same category as respect, because respect requires consideration (RECIPROCITY) and TRUST can be that consideration. If I don't respect you, I don't TRUST you. When you respect someone, they have earned your TRUST. The best way to build TRUST, which can also build respect is "to match your words with your actions". The only thing I have in business is my word, which earns my reputation. Reputation is how someone else sees you, but RESPECT is also a reflection of how you see yourself.

African American women have been put down so many times by so many people that it is hard for us to hold our heads high. Just recently, I was on the train speaking to the woman next to me and telling her my story of weight loss. She asked me if I loved myself more as a size ten and I said "No, I love myself the same". I still see myself as the little fat girl in the room and actually are surprised when people look at me. This is what made Islam so attractive to me. It is the veils and garb that are designed to protect women and hold women in high-esteem. Unfortunately, society places value on women based on how they look.

Islam, my chosen religion as of April 3rd, 2010, gives great importance to marriage. Re-reading "Relationships 101" in my new place, where God may be preparing me for marriage by placing the same consideration of my business relationships to my family, has changed my definition of success. "Success at home means all other relationships become easier." Here is a quote from Nick Stennet Family Life Expert: "When you have a strong family life, you receive the message that you are loved, cared for and important. The positive intake of love, affection and respect give you inner resources to deal with life successfully." I know I have a lot on my plate, and God made a way through the Religion of Islam for me to accept a help-mate. My clients and I base our pride on the ability to get things done, and I understood from the moment my third child was born that I could not do everything by myself. It was a BFF's Islamic family as my role model on the love and commitment that is needed to raise children in a two parent household.

Now that I have the understanding of what it is needed on my end to have strong relationships, I have to find or teach others how to do the same. This will breed a new generation of people who know how to communicate effectively and build the bonds that reverse the alarming trends of single motherhood that disproportionately affect the African American community. This was written so we can share and dialogue about how to assemble effective relationships that build communities which start with loving two parent families at home. To all my sisters holding down the fort at home like me may Allah make it easy on you, and I LOVE YOU!

"Wisdom is knowing the right path to take and integrity is it."
M.H.McKee

Chapter 5: Integrity

It's hard to even talk about integrity without first understanding what I will call, "one's person take on things." Many people would call it "their Philosophy". Philosophy defined is the rational investigation of the truths and principles of being, knowledge, or conduct.

When you attempt to learn yourself, what you are really doing is figuring out what people call 'your philosophy'. September of 2009, I paid $3,000 to attend a four day class to learn how to grow my business by learning why I am the way I am, and that was the key to unraveling my person take on things. I seek truth and view teaching and learning as one in the same. I learn so I can teach and I teach so I can learn.

Growing up, I was angry at how unfair the world could be. Whenever something would happen, I would always say "that is not fair" and my mom would counter back, "Life is not fair," and under my breath (because you know I did not dream of talking back to my mom), I would say, "Life is not fair, but you should be." My personal take on things, from the time I read it in the 6th grade, is the golden rule: "treat others as you would want to be treated". I was not born into a religion, so I studied different religions in college and this golden rule is universally applied from Islam to Christianity, to Jainism, Hinduism and beyond. It is the ethic of reciprocity. The law of reciprocity is the driver of my integrity.

Integrity from Webster's dictionary is firm adherence to a code of especially moral or artistic values. In graduate school, we took a business ethics class where we visited the federal prisons and talked to prisoners of white collar crimes. I would agree with my guide, John C. Maxwell, that there is no such thing as business ethics, there is only one rule in making decisions (the golden rule). My take on things guides my integrity, which is the moral ground I stand on to make decisions for me. Even before the issue is addressed, my integrity has already determined the decision. I remember reading stories about how people did not borrow money because they wanted to be sure they could pay it back, so they only operated with cash. There were people who would rather die than not be able to pay backs their debts. It is very sad that in 2009, there are business owners who believe they can grow a business without addressing their credit. Your credit score is how life scores your integrity. It is impossible to become a wealthy business owner without paying your debts. Life experience shows that you don't get blessed with more until you take care of what you have.

As I talked about in my last chapter, starting a business on a shoe string budget (because minorities have yet to overcome the biases in the commercial lending industry) messed up my credit, but I am focused enough to understand that I have to have a plan to pay all those debts before I can grow my business! Are we out spending our tax refund check on the latest gadgets like new computers, TV's and cell phones, or are we making a plan to pay back those debts over time? If I want a million dollar business, I must also want a 700 credit score. The way you get to a million dollar business is borrowing money to increase capacity. To borrow money, your credit score must be credit worthy. Instead of serving 200 clients on Newman Networks[1], I want to be able to serve 2,000 clients, and that means being able to meet payroll from the IT dept., accounting dept., customer service dept., marketing dept., law dept. and HR dept., and to pay the lights, rents and utilities, until the 2,000 clients are in the network. I never said it was easy.

Integrity is not just present in credit, but it is found in your business and personal life. Being a female business owner has its own sets of challenges when it comes to working with men. As Sigmund Freud made famous, the sex drive is a source of human motivation and action. A lot of men have the mindset that women are only good for wives and lovers, not business. This philosophy flows into their integrity of treating women in business as accessories, i.e. nice to have but not really needed. I see this way too often when some men play the game of phone tag to see if I will chase or try to use their position as influence on my services, which does not work on me, or just won't show the common courtesy of "thank you ". I have learned to not take it personal; it is their philosophy of how they view women that is screwed. They are not purposefully working against Nicole Newman, they just haven't woken up to the opportunities that women in business possess.

Let me just wake a few of you guys up right now. These statistics come from the center for women's business research[2]. They say that 1.9 million firms are majority owned by women of color. Between 2002 and 2008, these firms grew faster than all other privately held firms. Female business owners will adopt to technology as a means to build workplace flexibility (I actually had to be a business owner – My daughter has karate practice at 2pm on Fridays). Male and female business owners have different management styles. Women emphasize relationship building as well as fact gathering and are more likely to consult with experts, employees and fellow business owners. And the most important, female owners of firms with $1 million or more in revenue are more likely to belong to formal business organizations, associations or networks than other female business owners (81% vs. 61%). Women, especially minority women are the fastest growing segment of entrepreneurs, and we network! Networking is what allowed us to raise our families, networking is what constructed the village, and networking is our *modus operandi*! It is what will make us strong.

Men network in the good old boys network. They have their group of ten guys whom they only do business with, while women interweave and network 50 strong. Women just network in bigger groups, and if you look at the executive directors of the non-profit organizations in Philadelphia, you will see that most of them are run by a women of color. This financial crisis the U.S. in will be saved by female business owners. The smart men are slowly but surely seeing the trends and aligning themselves with female business owners who are getting it done. As women network and net weave to get us out of this depression, all ships will rise but the tallest ships will be the ones where women and men are working together at the helm. Though we have 120 business owners already on Newman Networks[3] (over 85% percent of them are women), I challenge that there are more who are ready to change their philosophies and re-build their credit to build and grow our businesses collectively. Are you ready?

Chapter 6: March 10th, 1989

All I can say about 1986 – 1990 is that it was a blur. There was the Nicole who thought she was just too tough to be hurt before the incident, and then there was the reflective Nicole after. Before my life dramatically changed, I was living the high life; I had a little part-time job at Wendy's, and was finally able to afford the finer things in life . At that time it was Swatch shirts, Guess jeans and Gucci shoes. 1989 was going to be my year, I was going into my junior year at the High School of Engineering and Science, and on day two, had my first fight of the new year. Staci will tell that story later. We can laugh about it now, but at the time it wasn't funny. Staci and I were both suspended for three days, when I got back to school, the teachers thought I was a new student.

I fought every single year. I had to maintain my persona as a person not to be messed with, and on March 10, 1989, the persona turned on me. As I had the pleasure of speaking to Vare Middle School (thanks Tiye), 10th graders at Bartram High School (thanks Chandell) and young men at Project Great Potential (thanks Russell), wanted to know why my ex-best friend would stab me. Now it is time to share that story:

The story actually starts in October 1988. I sold a pair of gold earrings to my ex best-friend (let's call her Betty for this story) for $140.00. At the time, Betty was working, and because of our relationship, she was able to use the lay-away plan. She paid the initial deposit the first month, but after that I could not get in touch with her. Luckily, she went to Franklin Learning Center. At this time, the Broad Street Subway line would be packed with high school students. Central and Girls High students would get on first, a few students from Gratz, then my school HS of Engineering and Science, then the students from FLC and Ben Franklin all on our way to the 15th Street to catch the El up to our neighborhoods in West Philadelphia.

One day, I saw Betty on the subway and made it a mission to confront her about her outstanding balance. This particular day, there was a new group of girls who intervened on this quite obvious conversation about money. These girls, who I later found out were from the Behavioral Adjustment Center, demanded that she pay me the money owed.

So we just wind up talking smack that day, but Betty and about six of her friends came back the next day ready to battle. The girls from BAC were not expecting the attack, so they said showdown would be the next day. On the second day, at 15th street, a gang of 20 girls from BAC appeared ready to do battle. Now if you have 20 girls ready for a fight, something was going to happen. The adrenaline was so high that the girls just started getting into fights with anybody. For three months Betty did not appear at the 15th Street platform, and the girls from BAC were always on the lookout. So when she finally appeared in February 1989, it was on.

Betty and her friends fought with the BAC girls at 60th Street platform on that day, and Betty blamed me for the entire incident. As a result, Betty said she would no longer pay me the debt. Now I had a choice to make, I could have chose to walk away (it's only money), or to protect my reputation as a person not to be messed with. I made the choice to protect my reputation and that choice almost cost me my life.

Though I believe that everything happens for a reason, and that choice made me the person I am today, I am telling this story so that we can learn to make better choices tomorrow by learning from the mistakes we make today. I chose to go after the love of money before protecting my life. I have been asked to reflect how the choices we make everyday shape and mold our lives. The lesson I learned from that incident was that when we choose to pursue the goal of finances before anything else, we will always come up short.

Betty, who is about 5' 2" tall, must have thought that I had an unfair advantage (I am 5' 10" inches tall) in a fight, so she stacked the cards against me. I came to a fist fight and she came with a butcher knife. We arrived at 15th street (so there would be more room instead of the tiny platform of the sub), with our adrenaline very, very high. It was so high that when I hit her, it did not even bother me that a knife was slashing into my face (just superficial wounds) or cutting chunks out of my skin on my left forearm. I was still continuing to hit. But it was not until the knife shot straight into my neck like the slots in the butcher knife holder and I had to pull it out of my neck and watch all the blood seep down on my hands and clothes did I really start to slow down. Losing that amount of blood started to make me dizzy and bring my 220 pound body down to the ground. I am not sure what happened at this point; Jannelle and Karina will have to fill in the rest of the story, but I remembered hearing the sirens and being carried on a stretcher through the steps at the famous meeting spot – the clothespin. This could only be a Philadelphia story.

When I arrived at the hospital and went to the emergency room, it was a scene straight from ER, there was a team of people – doctors and nurses asking me questions while trying to assess the situation. I remember seeing on my mom's look of tragedy as she was forced to come and see her baby sitting cut up in a hospital bed.

In that moment, Nicole Newman could no longer be the tough persona I showed the world. I had to be the person who cared about me. I had now learned that my time on this earth is limited. Tomorrow is not promised. Every day, I should spend time on the things and the people who are the positive sources of energy, and not waste precious time with people and things that are draining resources. It is spending time and loving me that recharges my batteries.

My mom likes to say that God will give you a gentle shove to guide you in the right direction. When a person fails to heed, He gives a greater punch, and when a person fails to heed that, He will knock you down. For me, it took three knock down punches for me to wake up. This first punch was my ego. Now I had to go back to school and face the people I had fought, and choose to walk with my head held high or walk with my back slouching low. Betty had cut with her knife the thing that women have cherished, the face. A woman's face shows the beauty that lies beneath the surface, and my face had been scarred, bruised, and beaten, but I had a choice to look at myself in the mirror everyday and begin to thank God for sparing me my life. When I could measure the broken skin and the stitches holding it together to the fact that I was even fortunate enough to live that day, then I could walk back into school and face my foes with my head held high.

Now it was not a cake walk, as I did not venture down to the 15th street platform for a quite some time. My dad came and picked me up every single day from school. I went home, and out of sheer boredom, picked up the books and did what I should have been doing all along: my homework. Because I no longer would allow myself to be distracted by social pressures, my grades phenomenally improved. The lectures did not get to me but the force of life itself being taken shook up my world.

Out of this experience, I also got a lesson on the unfair system that operates under the hypocritical name of the "Justice system". My junior prom was sometime in May, and on that day, two police officers showed up at my school to arrest me, but I was not at school. Betty said that I had jumped her in the first altercation with the girls from BAC. That Monday, I had to turn myself into the 55th and Pine St. police precinct. As I was being fingerprinted, I noticed that my arresting officer happened to be my girlfriend's mom (even then, Philadelphia could be easily connected). We were fortunate; my mom had the advantage of being able to write a $500 check that day and hire an attorney on retainer. It was that incident that taught me that money is access. Money is just the mechanism to access people, and it might be said that people are the best sources of information. The attorney could therefore respect my family as clients because we respected his law degree and experience by providing compensation for his services. I will gladly pay $500 to a membership to the Greater Philadelphia Chamber of Commerce to get access to 5,000 members. My value ratio is $500 divided by 5,000 members. That is just ten cents a connection! Now, does the chamber automatically give me access? No, but we have a common connection.

Even though I was the one with the wounds, the judge found me guilty. But I knew the outcome before we even stepped in court. The city was forced to make examples out of us because we were causing a great disruption on the El platform. Justice is not blind. The justice system is affected by what goes on in the world. Judges read papers too!. That is why I was attracted to Pre-paid Legal services as a network marketing company. I had been a card carrying member even before I found out it was a network marketing opportunity. I had been caught up in the justice system and seen that there is no incentive to do the right thing. The incentive is to get through the case load, to move up political aspirations, and hope the right cases outweigh the wrong cases.

What kept me out of the jail cells and on probation was my track record. My grades that I got (or the accounting books that I keep) are a timeline of our ability to do the right thing. That is why I have been asked to get rid of the hustle mode we have in business. Hustle mode is staying under the radar by not filing taxes, under-reporting income, not getting a business license, not incorporating or working the business as a way to stash cash without bank accounts which can never equate to wealth. I will gladly work to do the accounting, budgeting and keeping our credit straight, because I know these are the vital steps to laying a foundation for business. That track record allowed my company to get certified, and then, show that Newman Networks[4] can grow 100 clients through building relationships in the first year, build a system to grow 500 clients through relationships and resources in subsequent years to grow their businesses and duplicate the system. Then manage 2,500 clients through relationships, resources, synergy later on. We will have developed sustainable long-term businesses that will break us out of the financial depression and into wealth and abundance. It has been written that there is the right model of working collectively and using team work to generate an accountability system with checks and balances to build sustainable businesses. We each have a choice, but alternatives lead to spinning wheels without going anywhere fast. When I was judged on that day over 20 years ago, I had a school transcript very similar to my profile on my LinkedIn.com to show the quality of the person that was being judged.

That is why my grades went from a C's to A's. We don't just get judged just when our time on this earth is up. We are judged on a daily basis by clients, co-workers, friends and lovers. The best way I have seen to be judged positively is to bring something or someone constructive into our clients, co-workers, friends and lovers lives. Can we look in the mirror of our scarred, bruised and battered faces and know that we can walk with our heads held high even in the face of foes because we are doing the right thing? That one moment in time allowed me to take off the mask of the tough girl and show the beautiful spirit that glows from knowing Nicole Newman is working on building the model of wealth and abundance for you...

Sadie Tanner Mossell Alexander (January 2, 1898 – November 1, 1989), was the first African-American to receive a Ph.D. in economics in the United States, the first woman to receive a law degree from the University of Pennsylvania Law School, and the first national president of Delta S gma Theta Sorority, Incorporated. She practiced as an attorney from 1927 to 1982. She was the first African-American woman appointed as Assistant City Solicitor for the City of Philadelphia. She was not the first in her family. Her father was the first African American to graduate from University of Pennsylvania Law School, and his brother, Nathan Francis Mossell (1856–1946), was the first African American to graduate from the University of Pennsylvania Medical School. She was awarded the Francis Sergeant Pepper Fellowship, enabling her to continue her studies and in 1921 became the first African-American woman in the United States to earn a Ph.D. She was the first African-American woman admitted to the University of Pennsylvania Law School. In 1927, she was its first Afr can-American woman

graduate, and the first to be admitted to the Pennsylvania Bar. INSPIRATION!

Chapter 7: An Educated Sista

One of the hardest decisions in my mother's life (I think) was the decision to let me go. As a teenager, I was on a path of self-destruction, and no one, not even my mother, could get in the way. For some reason (hormones, growing pains), I became unruly and disrespectful. When I was 16, I got myself into what I will call "a financial situation". Since it was not my first "financial situation", my mother decided that I needed to resolve it myself.

Since I was in the 8th grade, I found myself in at least one "altercation" per year. Violence is what happens when people don't have an intelligent way to win an argument. I vividly remember in the 9th grade during the last two weeks of school, I received three pink slips from three different teachers. I was suspended from school for three days. You would think I learned something from that experience, but in the 10th grade, at the very beginning of the school year, I found myself yet again in another "altercation", and was suspended for another three days. This "altercation" happened on Temple University's property. My foe, who is now one of my closest BFF's, tells me that we were detained by Temple police for making an "altercation" on Temple's property. I still don't remember this at all since I am trying really hard to block this whole incident from my memory.

The 11th grade "altercation" also occurred at the beginning of the school year. This "altercation" resulted in a three day suspension and one of my teachers upon my return to school thought I was a new student. In 11th grade I bumped the number of occurrences up to two per year. By this point, my mom was going gray from having to deal with all my issues. This was the time she had a choice to make. She tells me her options were to let me go or kill me. In the face of death, letting me go was such a better choice! At least she did not kick me out; she still provided a roof over my head. My mom says that since I was going to act like I was grown, I had to learn to be responsible like I was grown. It was the 11th grade year when I found myself in a time sensitive "financial situation" and I asked my mom for help. She said no. You got yourself into this "situation", you will have to get yourself out of it. So here I was, 16 years old with no job, no support and no money trying to figure out what to do.

The United States is a capitalistic (money, resources) society, with capital you can do just about anything (does not apply to minorities - see Michael Vick or Michael Jackson or the countless other African - American males imprisoned at astronomical rates in the correctional facilities). I must have been born an entrepreneur because even then I was resourceful. I called at least 20 places in the tri-state area asking for help, and found a loan program to borrow the money to get me out of my "financial situation". That "can do" attitude is what makes me an educated sista MashaAllah. It is not my degrees, it is not my street address, it is not designer clothes nor a pair of Jimmy Chou or Manolo Blahnik shoes that makes one educated. It is the ability to collect data, turn it into information, make a decision and execute on that decision.

Just like Jay-Z, I had Ego and Pride. Going through that experience made me believe that, not only do wonders happen, but also that the unexpected is possible, and that much of life is what I make it. My new slogan in life became "If it was meant to be, it is up to me". Now my slogan is, "Whatever Allah willed to be shall be and whatever Allah did not will to be shall not be". *Repetition is a good teacher, and if I wanted to stop getting into "situations", I had to think differently.*

It is beautiful, intelligent brain that I have been blessed with that makes me an Educated Sista. An Educated Sista knows the importance of learning (religion, in school, out of school, on the job, in the streets), and she uses that knowledge to uplift and inspire others through community building organizations. African Americans, as a collective group, are doers but as a collective group we are not organized. The money, clout and respect come through using our collective resources to organize by the laws and corporate structures of the United States which set the foundation to initiate change. We have to stop depending on the same system that enslaved us to free us.

It was network marketing that taught me, as it is sometimes said, that one plus one does not equal two, but it equals 11. As my favorite recording artist besides Michael Jackson, Ne-Yo said in the song *Make me better*,: "I'm a movement by myself, but a force when we're together. Mami, I am good all by myself, ooh baby you make me better, you make me better."

Let me give you just a few examples of uneducated sistas:

Uneducated sistas stay in unhappy relationships for convenience.

Uneducated sistas don't learn to value themselves.

Uneducated sistas are waiting for someone to help a sista out AT THE SAME TIME unwilling to help themselves.

Just today, I had a female client call me twice while I was at a conference in Washington DC waiting for a phone number that was readily available on the internet or in a phone book. This is an example of a sister who is waiting for someone else to provide knowledge instead of seeking knowledge herself, and one day being in the best position of providing knowledge to others.

I also had a female client with an MBA tell me that she does not need my consulting services because she knows what to do. She said her business suffers from cash flow or time. She does not even realize that the knowledge and connections I have could get her up to five part-time employees for FREE, to expand her operations, and increase her bottom line.

An Educated Sista knows that EVERYONE has knowledge and seeks that knowledge from multiple sources. To ALL my sistas, STOP! STOP, waiting for some man, a check from the government, your job, or a "miracle" to change your situation and make you feel good. My mother taught me this skill, and this skill I am determined to pass to my children. It is the skill of "D.I.Y." Do It Yourself. It is my job to prepare them for the harsh realities of adulthood by providing them with the framework of "I SEEK KNOWLEDGE". I seek knowledge from family, friends, enemies, books, internet, podcasts, some TV but not too much and the trials and tribulations they will face in life. For me, every experience has a nugget of knowledge, and it is for me to question, evaluate and analyze the experience to see how I can overcome the challenge the next go round. I have seen that life presents the same experiences until you learn to overcome.

I give thanks to Allah for blessing me with my mom who gifted me the skill of D.I.Y. at the young age of 16. That incident empowered me and made me a seeker of knowledge. One of my clients told me recently that a person who can't say "YES" to your request is also a person who can't say "NO" to your dreams. When you are presented with fear and shadows of doubt, turn to your Educated Sista's who will inspire, motivate and provide you the framework to get to your destination of success in overcoming this challenge which will prepare you for the next challenge.

I love my Educated Sista's for working collectively through organizations "To be the change we want to see in the world."

Chapter 8: Sucker FREE

Philadelphia can be a tale of two cities, on the right hand we are the city of brotherly love, and on the left hand we are the murder capital of the world. I have been stabbed, punched, beat up, and robbed by my fellow neighbors, who at the same time, take my trash out every week and clean my yard without receiving a dime in compensation for the past six years. I have had the pleasure of meeting the nicest people here and building a network of close friends and associates who fuel my business. What scares most Philadelphians, and to a larger extent, most people, is being labeled as a "sucker", which I no longer fear.

A sucker is a person who is gullible and easy to take advantage of. Many a person is a sucker at some point in his life. We are born unprotected, needing others to guide us, feed us, and shelter us emotionally and physically. We are born vulnerable. When we are vulnerable, we are easy to be taken advantage of, and that is why it is so disturbing when adults prey on the children. Childhood is not easy for the urban community. Too many people in close quarters results in a breeding ground for violence. If you have the privilege of making it through childhood, you have the privilege of walking into adulthood, where racism, sexism and the other various forms of discrimination (based on citizenship, age, religion, and this list could go on) hit you like a ton of bricks right in the face. Women especially feel it in their pocketbook, because even in 2008, based on the studies by the Institute for Women's Policy Research, The median weekly earnings of female full-time workers was $657, compared with male median weekly earnings of $819. Based on this data, the ratio of women's to men's median weekly earnings was 80.2. Women are still receiving just 80 cents to a man's dollar. As I was buying services from one of my female business clients, she said that she was not taking me on as a client for the money, but for the relationship. I quickly told her that was the wrong attitude. You will be shown how you are valued based on how people buy AND PAY for your services. Money is an exchange of VALUE and females in this country do not command the same value as men. Smart men know that women could make better workers because PRIDE does not get in their way when it comes to getting the job done. Historically, since women don't demand the same pay scale as men, women have a higher productivity ratio (work/cost) per worker (i.e. she puts in more work and gets paid less for the work). That is why some men who own companies prefer to have an all female or mostly female workforce. A female work force will produce more and not have the EGO issues that many men bring into the workforce.

Now we have survived childhood, made it into the workforce, and are ready to make a commitment to the greatest institution in the world, the institution of marriage. In our Religion, marriage is an institution by which families can be lawfully built. However, this is a quote from Wikipedia on marriage: "One of the oldest known and recorded marriage laws is discerned from Hammurabi's Code, enacted in ancient Mesopotamia (widely considered as the cradle of civilization). Various cultures have had their own theories on the origin of marriage. One example may lie in a man's need for assurance as to paternity of his children. He might therefore be willing to pay a bride price or provide for a woman in exchange for exclusive sexual access. Legitimacy is the consequence of this transaction, rather than its motivation. In Comanche society, married women work harder, lose sexual freedom, and do not seem to obtain any benefit from marriage. But nubile women are a source of jealousy and strife in the tribe, so they are given little choice other than to get married. "In almost all societies, access to women is institutionalized in some way so as to moderate the intensity of this competition."

I read a discussion just yesterday on linkedin.com. A man said, "I reminded my wife today that our marriage is 50/50". She was inclined to agree with me, as long as I understood that her half equals 80%. It is institutionalized in most western societies that women become assets of a man, and are expected to be more productive and get paid less. My reply to the discussion was, "And that is why I remain single!"

Now let's say a person starts a business, buys real estate or becomes an entertainer, then the vultures eye their prey. From answers.com, a vulture is a person of a rapacious, predatory, or profiteering nature. Business, real estate and entertainment all have the ability to generate positive cash flow, and human nature dictates that people smell money and vulnerability (i.e. SUCKERS). Many people, women and men, will get taken advantage of at some point. That is just part of the game (see any Jay-Z song in which he blasts the recording industry). What is important is to learn the lesson by changing the circle of business partners and move on (see the story of DiversePhilly.com). No business, entertainer or real estate mogul grows by himself; we all need each other to grow, but business principle's tell us to implement a check and balance system. The accountant can't have cart blanche to the bank account, the company should have a board of advisors.

Then each person, regardless of race, can be held responsible and accountable to each other. For any of that to happen, TRUST (the capacity for trusting, the perception of competence, and the perception of intentions) must be developed in the communication and shared experience process. Personally, I can be brutally honest. Not only can I dish it, but I am strong enough to accept responsibility and take it. Many people say my honesty makes me vulnerable, but I believe honesty is my strength. Honesty is the building block of my company. I have seen money come and go, I have seen possessions come and go, I have seen knowledge come and go. My relationships start out as trustworthy and through time that trust is usually broken. It is usually broken by people who are out to intentionally or unintentionally think of the other party as prey. Business (and marriage) is not dog-eat-dog. Business (and marriage) is about personal development and communication skills. To attract a network of like-minded individuals to build a (business) professional and (marriage, friendship) personal relationship, I require honesty, integrity and a SMART (specific, measurable, attainable, realistic and timely) goal for the relationship. Just like in any business which can then be applied to personal, a goal will keep your relationship moving forward. The goal should be the passion of both parties and an 'expectations conversation' will set the stage for the roles and responsibilities of each party.

Worrying about being labeled "a sucker" will keep me from reaching out to the like-minded individuals who can be brutally honest and provide the constructive feedback I need to achieve SMART goals. If the trust is broken, I say what lesson can I learn, apply the lesson, and move on. My motto is not "Don't Worry, Be Happy" but "Don't Worry, Make Money". Now it is my time to start living - sucker FREE!

Nicole's Commentary (2009)

My children are great teachers. Omar, the middle child, lives in the 'OR' world. He is always asking, "Is it red or blue?" "Can I have an apple or an orange?" When there is nothing to compare, he adds - OR NOT to make a comparison. He will ask, "Can I play on your computer or not?" Nasir, my youngest child, lives in the 'AND' world. If I ask, "Do you want a pretzel or a water ice?" He will say, "I want a pretzel AND a water ice." He wants it all; there is never a choice for him. Our Saturday routine involves going to the corner store and getting donuts (that way the kids can stop asking for donuts Monday through Friday). Omar wanted the mini donuts from the store. I asked Nasir, "Do you want the mini-donuts or a big donut?" He said "I want the mini donuts AND a big donut." I said, "You can only have one." So he thought for a while and he said, "I want a big donut."

Even though I said this to him, I know in my heart that I too live in the 'AND' world. I want a profitable AND a socially conscious company (see triple bottom line with social venture institute). I want to run my own company AND be a part of a team. I want to be a mentor to teach AND a mentee to learn. I want a traditional business AND a network marketing business. I want to stay connected to my heritage AND be able to work with everybody. I want to be a career woman AND a work at home mom. Being an entrepreneur is the only way I could achieve the time and freedom to teach and learn from my children AND the financial freedom to build generational wealth. Being a member of both the African American Chamber of Commerce AND the Greater Philadelphia Chamber of Commerce allows me to tap resources from inside AND outside of my community to achieve this goal.

I bought Omar and Sahar, my daughter, the mini donuts. Nasir found a smart way to get everything he wanted. He got a mini donut from his big brother and his big sister and the big donut for himself. In essence, he is just like me, and he got it all - That's my boy!

It is easier to build strong children than to repair broken men."
Fredrick Douglass

There are many men who contributed greatly to our success and introduced me to Jawala Scout so my sons would experience men being active in the lives of OUR youth. But in my neighborhood, young men celebrate birthdays by drinking and smoking marijuana WITH their parents! It takes a man to raise a man which is why I am so disappointed by father's not being an active part of their children's lives (hence we have lost boys)....

Chapter 9: The Lost Boys

My children ARE among my greatest teachers. They teach me all the habits (good and bad) that I show them. When I was called into entrepreneurship, I asked, "Why now?" Why would you call me when I am trying to raise a four year, three year old and a one year old? We were called because we were ready to learn. My children hold me accountable to demonstrate good habits so they can learn from the model I build. As I have seen, each of my children have a different part of my personality in them.

Sahar (meaning dawn), my little princess, is innocence. Even when she is only seven she has become such a helper to me as I struggled to juggle the duties of mom, dad and business owner. With all the negativity she sees on TV, she refuses to participate. She recognized that I value her smarts. When we are riding in the car, she frequently challenged me to math and spelling questions so she can sharpen her skills. She is always looking to please. She is a smart girl who is willing to work at being book smart. Just like me, she does not value street smarts.

Street smarts (or lack thereof) got me stabbed in my face, neck and left arm at the young age of 16.

Nasir meaning protector and victory is charm. Nasir is my baby boy, and he is liked by everyone he meets. He has a beautiful smile and is cute as a button. Nasir knows how to use his smile to get what he wants which is usually food. He gets all attention from not only me but his big brother and his big sister.

Omar meaning long-lived is my middle child. I knew from before he came out of my womb, he would be special. Omar has the spirit of two children (read Chapter 12 – discipline). Like his brother before him, he was born with the cord around his neck, but unlike his older brother, Shawn, he survived. As a very rare O negative child who is G6PD deficient, I was correct, he is special. At two weeks, Omar was strong enough to lift his head up. At four weeks he could roll over. He has enough energy for two children, and I credit that with having a heavy load. My job as a parent is to prepare my children with the skills to survive in this world. It was Omar that made me find an environment in which he could prosper. My children went to the cyber charter school[6] so they could learn at their own pace and stay in school from eight am to five pm. Most parents home school their children who attend but there are a few fac ities that facilitate cyber charter curriculum. Even though I have three children, they all have different personalities and need different skills to survive. All of the children are smart, but Omar is mentally gifted. Omar likes his independence and has a hard time getting focused. Just like an entrepreneur, he needs to know a return on investment for spending time in his education. Though he is smart, he loses focus very fast and is bored easily with mundane school work assignments.

Unfortunately, I understand too well that our school systems, our corporate structures and our families are failing our children, particularly, our boys. I knew that before I had sons and in the last year, I have seen all those structures fail Omar. Omar has a special bond with my father. As I have stated in Chapter One (Daddy's Little Girl), my father failed me as a parent and sometimes becoming a grandparent allows them a chance to make up with their children, but my dad has failed his grandchildren. Even though my father lives less than two miles from me, we have not seen or spoken to him since what they call "Christmas" day.

My father used to do the same thing to me. Every Christmas he would come by for ten minutes just to drop off presents, but I would not see him again for another year, and by the end of Christmas day I would be so mad that that I would give away all his gifts. What I really needed from him was his time and attention.

Now I say we are failing our boys, because of the way we treat our daughters as princesses but our sons like trash. I was my mother's only child and my sons are a handful, but my mom has a habit of spending more time with my daughter than both my sons combined. Although girls are her comfort zone, it is unfair to discount what her attention means to the boys. Omar now has taken a negative attitude. Nasir doesn't get that affected because he gets attention from everybody all the time, but this means Omar, the middle child, has to act out to garner some. That is why he gets the most attention from me. I am trying to feed Omar the love he is supposed to receive from his grandfather, his grandmother and his dad.

My son's father has failed as a parent, but I think that is just a reaction. There is a deeper issue lurking, and that is why their father has left me with the almost impossible task of teaching a boy how to become a man. Even at the young age of five, my son has lost his innocence. I guess because of all of the systems families, education and hormones breaking down and failing on him. I am watching his ascent into adolescence as he tries to deal with the hormones that have awaken inside. Looking at him now, I see a man unlike his younger brother popping through.

Even the cyber charter school system has failed him. Our first facilitation center sent me home with a note in October stating effective immediately we were no longer welcomed there. For a whole month, we sat in limbo as I tried to find a facility suitable for two children with different personalities and different needs. From December until March, I had three children in three different schools. This was Omar's first year in kindergarten, and since the school did not want to have a failing student as he missed a month of learning on their record; in March, I received a note saying the school had withdrawn my son from the school. The net effect is training for high school dropouts, who are measured in the third grade, for entry into institutionalized court/prison system. We have built a system in which to train our African American males to the next form of slavery, prisons. Slavery is defined from Webster's dictionary, as the state of a person who is a chattel of another. In this case, the "another" is Corporate America who buys time from the prison system without compensation to the prisoner's doing the work.

Last week, I received a note stating that Omar bit another child and then on Monday he actually hit another child in anger over a toy. I vividly remember having that same burning fire in my soul, and only through entrepreneurship did I get to fully release it. It happened to me as a teenager, but in the fast paced world of today, I see it in my growing child. The administrator thought it would be beneficial to have a conference with both parents and I reluctantly agreed. It was at the meeting that I saw how we toughen our girls while softening our boys. I know when Omar is acting out that what he is asking for is love. Among the greatest things I can do for my children is to love them unconditionally. Studies have shown that a child hears "No" 148,000 times, but only hears yes a few thousand times[7].

Every day, Nasir asks for and gets a hug. Though Omar does not ask for a hug (he is the tough man), he needs one just the same. Sahar rarely asks for a hug, but she makes sure she gets her attention. She knows no matter what I do all day long, she is sleeping in my bed at night. She had been in that bed since she jumped out the crib at eight months old. At the conference, I explained to Omar that it was not okay to hit, and he should tell the teacher when someone hits him. I said this to him as I gently hugged him and watched his body relax and take just three seconds to bring his wall down and let a single tear drop before wiping his eyes and replace on the mask of being a man. THIS REALLY HAPPENED AT THE YOUNG AGE OF 5. Now the other child's mom got very upset and tried to disrespect me by saying I don't discipline my children and her child would never hit anybody. She went on to say that my children should know this is kindergarten not pre-k (even now that makes me chuckle). As I looked at her and laughed, she got mad. I asked her when should they know that they are not in pre-k anymore? (It is still funny), I said I got stabbed when I was 16. I guess the girl that stabbed me should have known we were not in pre-k anymore.

She looked at me and said she did not appreciate my reaction to the severity of the situation. See that same negative reaction got me stabbed in the first place. I said apparently you are mad and I don't talk to people when they are in that state of mind. This happened in front of our children and now we have taught them they don't have to be responsible for their actions.

Now if we are teaching them to shy away from their responsibilities at five, can we get mad at the petty crimes committed at 10? Can we get mad at the drug dealing street life at 13? Can we get mad at the incarceration by 18? We are steady in feeding the prison system mind shackled, uneducated boys in our refusal as parents to deal with our issues. While we shuffle the children from school to activities to homework to bed, are we feeding them the life nuggets of understanding and caring that are needed in this world. I know I am not the best role model, but I know that my child is failing, not because he can't do the work, but he has no value in the work, because we as a community are failing to value him. He doesn't need a tutor, he needs parents and grandparents that LOVE him. I can't believe their father has the audacity to walk out on these innocent lives in my children but turn around and ask for me for a Facebook connection request! Where is the love? When are we going to stop trying to heal the scar with classes, programs and non-profit organizations but fix the wound by just breaking bread and spending time with our children and valuing them? When are we going to look inside ourselves and figure out how to give not toys or presents but gifts of unconditional love that cannot be brought again and find the pure joy that giving unselfishly can bring?

As I now have to break down my wall to wipe a single tear from my eye, I am learning the lesson that only motherhood can bring - the lesson of seeing yourself in the reflection your children are to you. I was once that child who craved love and now I have to watch my son become another who is craving love. We have to change this cycle, we have to take responsibility for our collective community. We have to appreciate and give back to the environment that made and built us. I write this book to affect parents to see the signs of an unloved child crying for help. But this is not a job for one person, this is a job for the community to mentor each other, to give and rebuild institutions, to show what are our proper roles as parents, mentors, brothers, husbands, wives in society. My children reinforce the idea that we have to take responsibility. Omar is energy that drives me to get it done. If I fail in my business then I will be another institution that has failed him. Omar – if God took me away today, know that I worked my best to not fail you. You are truly a gift and mommy will be your foundation for love. I LOVE YOU...

Nicole Newman is not wasting time! I go after people who want to change and don't waste my time or their time with those who don't. They say - "There are only two times, NOW and TOO LATE". For me, the time is NOW to make that change.

Chapter 10: The Transformation

The only constant in life is change. For me, there are two beliefs that keep me grounded: understanding that life is about our ability to react to change, and everybody and I mean EVERYBODY has benefit for a long time, I thought life was about me. Though my mom and I did not grow up materially wealthy, I can say that I had everything I needed, and I was fortunate to get a lot of what I wanted.

My lifestyle as a child is very similar to the lifestyle I want as an adult, and the lifestyle I want to teach my children. My earliest memories are from growing up in the Wynnefield section of the city. Then we moved to West Philadelphia, 406 North 63rd Street to be exact, where I met my first love, Tony. Then we moved to 61st and Walnut Streets, and this is what I claim as home. After that, we headed to "the Bottom", 34th and Baring. We made a pit stop at my mom's BFF's house on 55th and Arch. We moved about every three years. By the time I left for college we were living on 34th Street, and when I came back we had moved on up, like the Jefferson's, to Chelsea on Ridge Avenue. Then we stayed in a rooming house in Germantown.

That was a pit stop on our way to North Philadelphia/Fairmount .Fairmount is the fancy term for North Philly at 21st and Corinthian Streets. I have fond memories of the daily walk to Temple University, for that is how I lost weight the first time. Now it was time for us to move to 5th and Poplar in North Philly/Northern Liberties. What is wrong with just calling it like it is – North Philly?. After I started college, I continued our family tradition of "Keeping It Moving".

College started for me at University of North Carolina at Greensboro. My second year, during fall break, I was involved in a car accident that left me with a hematoma which is wwelling of blood in the brain and a broken femur bone. Why did I have to break the largest bone in the body? I stayed in the University Of Virginia Medical Center for ten days and tried unsuccessfully to finish my semester at UNCG. Upon returning to Philadelphia, I finished college at Temple University (TU!) and lived in three different off-campus apartments (North Philly, North Philly, then South Philly) in three years...

Claymont, DE

You would think that I understood my life was about change, but at that time I thought I wanted to settle down, so at the age of 22, I bought my first house in Claymont, Delaware... I was at the settlement table when my realtor told me a great secret that I will share with you: the earlier a person buys real estate in life, the wealthier they will become. Real Estate is how wealth is buildd in this country. Most people don't use this wealth-building vehicle because they only by a house for their family needs. In Philadelphia, a city where a large percentage of the population rents – buying rental properties should be a no-brainer. I plan on making sure my children have at least three sheltered wealth building assets by the time they go off to college.

Living in Claymont, this was the very first time in my life that I had experienced darkness. Growing up in the city, I never knew that we don't really have darkness. On every city block there is a light to deter criminal activity, and soon there will be a camera (Max Headroom is coming). I am glad for the experience but after a two year stint, the burbs is not for me... Nice place to visit but I have no ntentions of doing it again as I learned my lesson. Delaware was just a stopover to my second home in Prince George's County, Maryland, affectionately known at PG County. I fell in love with PG county from the moment I arrived - there is a vibe of excitement given off by all the entrepreneurs there. PG county has the highest per capita income for African-Americans in the country. I lived in three different apartments before purchasing my second house from HUD in District Heights, Maryland. I had started my search in January of 1999 while I was pregnant with my first child, Shawn Aaron Newman but did not go to settlement until July of 2000 as I prepared for my second child, a daughter named Sahar.

District Heights, MD

In the development where I lived, if you were to drive by at 1 p.m. in the afternoon, half of the homeowners would still be there. I would also say they have a large percentage of entrepreneurs. I bought the house for $122,000 and sold it three years later for 162,000; I went to settlement with $4,500. My mortgage was 1,100 (which is the same at 800 rent), and sold it for a net profit of $32,000. That is an 800 percent return on a $4,000 investment. That was all the proof I needed to learn that investing in Real Estate is a very smart move!

Change can be a good thing. Change of people and change of scenery gives a new perspective on life. I plan on continuing our family tradition of moving around, to give my children new people and different experiences in life. Entrepreneurship has greatly helped in this endeavor. We have been fortunate to grow up with a technology that allows us to meet new people from around the world everyday. It has become especially easy susing social media tools like Facebook!.

What I realize now is that I did not change because of me. My life had a destination that was mapped out before I was even born. We all have a duty to fulfill. The experiences gathered as a result of change were to prepare me, and many others, to come together and change the landscape of the place I love: Philadelphia. When I realized the benefit to mankind upcn embarking on such a venture, I questioned why now; why take on this task when I have three children in tow and my life was starting to settle down into a routine? It was because the time was right for us (NOT

JUST ME). There were others out there going through their own transformation, and we were preparing for our meeting of the minds. The change required a new president, big companies to fall, a financial depression, a new mayor, a new superintendent of schools, and new technology. We were preparing for the perfect storm!

For a two-year period (2004-2006), I was frustrated that my spirit was not being fulfilled in life. I knew there was more, but did not know what I needed to make the change appear in my life. So when I was introduced to network marketing, I found a new reason to get up every day. Once the mind expands, it cannot go back again, and Quixtar expanded my mind. My mind did not expand just to network marketing, but it expanded to a traditional business based on leveraging the internet through Newman Networks[8]. As I worked on my business plan, the plan actually told me not to do the business; that I had no unique value proposition, and anybody could go out and develop the same business. I had to transform my mind, body and spirit to prepare for the journey I was stepping into. Through the three year transformation of mind, body and spirit, I realize my most important relationship is my dedication to God. What I find interesting is that I was claiming to be an atheist at the time. Sometimes we lie to ourselves, and I was not really an atheist. I was just mad at everything I had gone through.

I had no idea that the stabbing in my neck by a "BFF", that the still birth experience with Shawn, and that the broken leg was all to prepare me for the most awesome journey one can imagine. Life is about your obedience to God and living life according to His Law. I had been a wild child, and every day I see the wild child in me come out through my son, Omar. But living my life under his rules has buildd a sense of calm and peace within my soul.

God's rules are wise. How I show my wisdom is by making your business better by using the same techniques used in my own business. I have been gifted with the task of bringing the people in your life to make it happen!

And what about LOVE? Most people use the word LOVE too loosely. There are things we admire and respect about people in our lives but do we truly love their essence (or are we actually learning what they

LOVE?). Allowing me to Love your business (by connecting you to tools and resources), lets me LOVE the same things you do. There are steps to our ascent to learning how to LOVE Unconditionally:

1. I had to SUBMIT to Allah subhuman wa ta^ala. Then I had to:

2. CHANGE. I Lost 72 pounds, embraced Islam, quit my J. O. B., (and that was actually the easy part).

3. Then I had to LOVE myself (warts and all). Even though I was 32 years old, I really did not know myself. I had not taken the time to write down what makes me tick. Why am I this way? Before you can LOVE yourself you must know yourself.

Then I had to LOVE others (I had to forgive people who had wronged me and learn to not take things so personally).

Being obedient to these steps allowed me the choice of ascending to the next level, where I can LOVE without the need for an intimate relationship. Being a woman in a male dominated field is challenging. A lot of men try to use their position to get sexual advances, and I just have to shrug my shoulders. I actually feel a little sad that they have not experienced the kind of LOVE that does not have a physical component. Being able to separate sex from love is how we learn to LOVE UNCONDITIONALLY. Most people do not have the pleasure of experiencing this level of LOVE because they neither love themselves nor value others (including the fathers who actually think there is nothing wrong with walking away from their children[I COULDN"T RESIST!]). Before we can love other people, we have to value them and the relationships they bring into our lives.

I'm living in amazement as I watch connections through people like Jim Smith who I met through a friend at Bright Hope Baptist Church, that put me on the path to write this book; or the Rochelle Davis, whose path I crossed by the collective goal of utilizing PEACE and LOVE to change the world. Or by an organization that is providing financing opportunities for Newman Networks[9] member's that I was introduced to through one of my BFF's, who introduced me to Valerie Ginyard, who introduced me to Michael Bing. I am honored to understand and be chosen as a follower for the awesome and transforming power of LOVE.

"Desire is the key to motivation, but it's determination and commitment to an unrelenting pursuit of your goal - a commitment to excellence - that will enable you to attain the success you seek."
Mario Andretti

Zig Ziglar said "It was character that got us out of bed, commitment that moved us in to action, and discipline that enabled us to follow through."

Chapter 11: Commitment

Why are we afraid of commitment?

I taught Social Media for Business to four students, although I received e-mails from at least 15 people saying they were going to attend. The four students who came had pre-registered for the class months in advance, unlike the 15 who just sent an email. Why are we afraid of commitment?

As I pondered this question, I looked up the word in the Merriam Webster's dictionary. Commitment is an act of TRUST. Ok, so that is why we are afraid. It is hard to put faith in the future. But for business ownership, failure to plan for the future is akin to being caught in complacency. There is no standing still in business; if we are not moving forward, we are moving backward.

It is running that taught me how to be in training mode and plan for the future. Today is the first day to register for the SheROX Triathlon on August 22nd, 2010. Though I don't know how to swim and haven't ridden a bike in years, I am registering and making both a financial and a time commitment in this future activity. It is time to stretch myself and move to the next level so I can lift the lid on my personal leadership skills (cc: John C. Maxwell - Leadership 101 and Sulaiman Rahman) and help more businesses navigate the road blocks in business ownership.

I found a great little article in my Google search, and it laid everything out in this one statement : "The most important single factor in individual success is COMMITMENT." My mentor, Sulaiman Rahman, likes to say that you have to practice little commitments to get to the big commitments. My business partner and I have an accountability call every single day. This is our journal of what we need to do for the day and it was her idea to add this activity to the schedule.I am committed to running four times a week, which translates into the business commitment of building a weekly (what is the schedule and what needs to get done), monthly (close the accounting cycle and publish the newsletters) and yearly (how many employees will we have, who are the strategic partners and what certifications do we need) list of what my business has to do to move forward. Sulaiman, I agree, it is those little commitments not just saying the words but doing the action which builds belief into completing bigger goals.

The article also states that commitment is demonstrated by a combination of two actions: supporting and improving. "Genuine support develops a commitment in the minds and hearts of others. This is accomplished by focusing on what is important and leading by example." It is my hope to show this by using and supporting businesses in the network and uncovering opportunities and new avenues to market their businesses with cost-effective marketing solutions.

The second action is improving. "Improving stretches our commitment to an even higher level. Commitment means a willingness to look for a better way and learn from the process." Though it was my dream to complete a triathlon, it started with a commitment to walk 1,000 steps a day, use what I learned to walk ten miles a week, then use what I learned to complete a 5K race which has lead me to register for the tri. Though we can never stop improving, this is where the fun is! My lifetime is not long enough to learn everything, so we must use our networks to shorten the learning curve and learn from each other!

That is why I am not afraic of commitment. I TRUST that I don't know everything and would be honored to learn from YOU! I will see the next group of students at the Social Media for Business class part II and COMMIT that the coffee is on me!

Since I have a lot of Facebook friends who don't know me (YET!), it is time to share a few more details about the product of my environment that God placed in the form of Nicole Newman. We have already covered my dad (Chapter one) who broke my heart from the very beginning, my grandmother (Chapter 2) who provided all the strength to deal with a broken heart, my BFF's (Chapter 4) who built the village for my family to do what we were called to do. This week has been a reflection of places I have come from and growing I have yet to do. I am on a mission to build a million-dollar enterprise, and in that mission discipline becomes your friend.

I am a constant planner. I believe in the quote, "Failure to plan is planning to fail." There are a lot of people who are planners but do not want to implement discipline required to stick to the plan. At one point in my life, I too did not have discipline as my friend. I remember I was a little girl maybe nine or ten years old, and my mom used to give me an allowance of four dollars a week. She said if I can save 15 dollars for the month she would double my 15 so I would have 30. Seems pretty easy, right? But at the end of the month, I had nothing. That childhood incident helps me understand why I now see discipline as my friend.

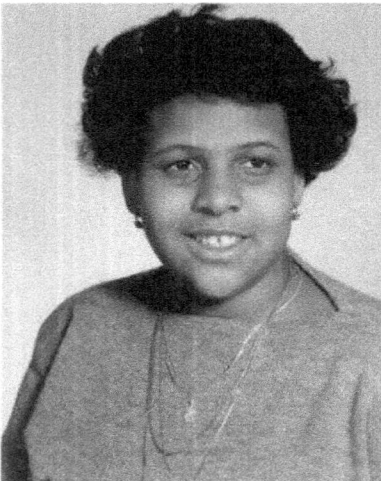

From the time I hit puberty to the age of 26, I was overweight. A normal weight from me was about 220 pounds, and when I was pregnant with my children, I averaged just shy of 250. While I attended the

University of Maryland College Park MBA program, I did lose a significant amount of weight, but did not have the discipline required to keep it off. The key to weight loss is understanding your body. We have to understand how weight is accumulated and how cells react to foods we eat. Not all calories are the same. What I learned the last time I lost weight was that weight loss is a lifestyle. The weight that my body finds comfortable requires a choice to add the discipline of eating breakfast every day, working out four times a week, and no carbohydrates after 6pm. Once I understood that principle, it became an easy choice to make. As Brian Williams and I talk about in the wealth building series, wealth is a habit of adding financial discipline to your life style. But most people don't get to financial discipline because they have not added discipline anywhere else in their lives.

Omar, my middle child, has always been the special one. My first son, Shawn was still born at eight months because the umbilical cord was tied around his neck. While I was pregnant with Omar (means long-lived in Islam), I vividly remember the day he turned to prepare for birth and I could sense that the cord was around his neck too. Since I already had a stillborn, I was classified as a high risk pregnancy. By this time, I was going for a checkup every three days. While I was there, we would sit on the monitor for 20 minutes and measure the heart rate, the placenta fluid and contractions if any. After Omar turned for passage through my womb, when I would have a contraction his heart would stop. That is why I named him Omar, it was my hope that he would be born and live a long-time. June 5, 2003, at my bi-weekly check-up, the doctor decided to induce my labor. My prayers were answered Omar R. Newman was born. The wild child in my stomach turned out to be just a wild child. He is a hyper active O-negative little boy and a vegetarian too! It was my four year old son who turned me on to becoming a vegetarian. Sahar and Nasir, Omar's brother and sister, think we are crazy; they are meat eaters!

Discipline can be thought of as tier-leveled habits. The discipline required to maintain a healthy body is just the first tier to build a better me. After I added exercise to my lifestyle, the discipline of vegetarianism was added as the next level. In order to build a million dollar business, we must add the financial discipline of budgeting and paying old debts to produce good credit as the next tier of discipline. I really don't know why people expect God to bless them with more when they are not taking care of the blessings already given. (O the irony! Did I mention I claimed to be an atheist until 2006? I really did believe in the existence of God though, I was just mad).

It is discipline that dictates my actions. Everything in my week is planned on Sunday. Sunday is when I focus my mind by God's will. While I am running at Valley Green (I can't wait until it gets warm outside) or attending services, Sunday is the day to clear my mind and start fresh on his goals. Discipline is involved when I am making the task list and checking of the tasks completed (I lost my list for two days and got nothing done. That won't happen again). It is now 12:30 AM, Saturday night, but I have a writing discipline of ensuring four pages of this book is written every week. Discipline can be involved everywhere in your life. My children know what time is bed time in the Newman household. They go to bed early on Friday night to get ready for the discipline of Saturday school the next morning.

Newman Networks[10] developed the wealth building series so we could learn what habits we need to generate enterprises. My dream is seeing what I saw when I lived in Prince George's County, Maryland: wealth and abundance. I saw people not go to a job, but were taking the responsibility to build a job. To attain wealth one must appreciate every day that we are given in this green earth to add value to it as opposed to taking away from it. The economic climate we have right now is because not enough of us are creating opportunities for others. The African American male unemployment rate is so high, the government refuses to talk about it[11].

We have to find another path for our youth to make it in the world or we will be doing what we have been doing: burying yet another young soul in the ground. The way to generate wealth is as simple as the time it takes to make a choice to spend that dollar on bling-bling or spend that dollar to invest in our collective future. The choice is yours.

My mentor, Sulaiman Rahman, taught me that all businesses need three beliefs in order to succeed: The business owner must have belief in the product, belief in the system and belief in himself. Newman Network's journey so far has been about uncovering how much I believe. When I started my company in 2006, and for a year in a half, I gave away our networking services for free. I learned that some business owners would still say no to free, but 80% will purchase a free product. How many will purchase the product at 15 dollars a month? How many customers will value my services? How much did I believe in me? Though I had belief in the Newman Networks[12] product, I had more belief in the system. I knew how to make a replicable system for business and my partner at EDSI (Operator of the PA sponsored EARN Center), could show business owners creative staffing solutions to implement the system. My belief is head strong, that a business is built on a legal, accounting, and marketing foundation. My belief is head strong that customer service, certifications (city, state and corporate) and all interactions with the customer fall under marketing. My belief is headstrong that business ownership is the key to building strong self-sustaining urban communities.

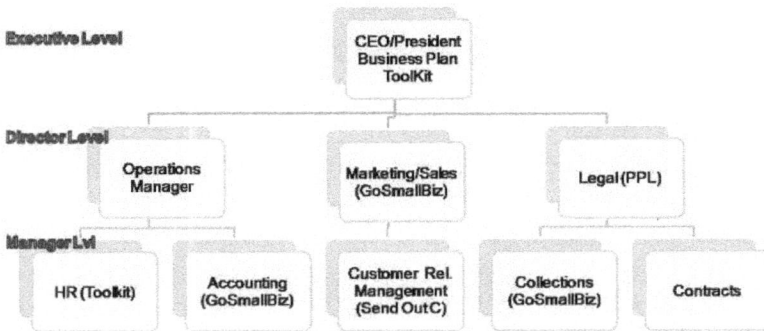

Business Systems Structure using web-based tools

My weakest belief was belief in me. In our Tuesday night training, my mentor would say, "Your income will never grow above your belief." You have to become wealthy in your mind with knowledge BEFORE wealth pours into your pockets. How do you become wealthy in your mind? By becoming a student and making a commitment to read 15 minutes a day. Reading everyday equates to finishing about one book a month. The hardest part was applying what I learned in the book to real situations. For almost a year, I avoided presenting my 30 second elevator pitch to my mentor. One day, he asked me to present and let's just say there was a lot of "constructive feedback". I knew that I had to go through it, and the very next week he asked me to present again. This time, my presentation was well received. Then I started to believe, (and my income grew as a consequence).

Over many years, I have had a revolving door of partners, some good and some very, very bad and other trusted counterparts looking for that synergy. In networking marketing, we say that one plus one does not equal two, it equals 11. Great things can happen when we play TEAM. As the saying goes, TEAMWORK makes the DREAM WORK. But just recently, as I went through a mini tail spin, I realized that I had my partner all along: The ever moving ambition that keeps us moving towards our goals, the spirit who saves us just in the nick of time.

I have a task, a challenge so great that I have to build years of trust and commitment from a team of like-minded entrepreneurs to fulfill the challenge. It is as if I have been chosen to be the economic stimulus package of Philadelphia, to align the various Chambers, Leagues and Community Development Corporations of Philadelphia that serve the business community, and to save a generation of young men from the prison system. He has enabled me to beat the obstacles of generations of single motherhood, poverty, obesity, hypertension, school violence, work stress and raising a family to OVERCOME. He has chosen me to be the one (as my mentor did for me) who BELIEVES in you.

I am the one...

I knew it...

I can't believe it...

I am truly blessed to understand...

The creative synergy is there.

The Love is there.

I had been living two lives:

Being the worker bee while the mind is trapped and getting just a little time to shine.

Thank you for allowing me to be.

Thank you for allowing her to come out.

Thank you for leading me to my rightful place in this world, and enabling me to uplift Newman Networks and allowing me:

To be the Businessman, Queen and Mother I need to be.

Thank you for allowing this independent woman to do:

Her duty as a WOMAN and submit my will to a one who guides.

I submit to you my GOD.

Do you believe?

Suicide is the absolutely lowest point of your self-esteem. According to a study by Philadelphia's own University of Pennsylvania[13], African American Males are 88% of all suicides in African American Youth. Suicide is the 3rd leading cause of death among African American Youth. There are 10.0 suicides among every 100,000 males and compared to 1.6 suicides among African American females. African American females are more likely to attempt suicide, but African American males are more likely to be successful. According to this study, African American Men (20.6 per 100,000) and almost as likely as white men (20.5 per 100,000) to complete suicide between the ages of 20-24. Unfortunately, my cousin did not see the warning signs that his 20 year old step-son was getting ready to complete his life. The step-son that he raised since he was four years old committed suicide last week.

My mom called me while I was learning how to make my business a million-dollar business in Secaucus, NJ to break the news. John, the straight A student had committed suicide and was found in his dorm room at the University of Connecticut. John had been a straight A student since he was in kindergarten. His parents made sure he stayed on the right track, but at college the flood gates of opportunities opened wide. He had to answer the two biggest questions in life – Who Am I and What am I here for. John went from being a clean shaven-straight A student to a flunking I don't care what happens beard and mustache man. The A's had quickly gone to F's. Two warnings signs of depression and suicide – loss of interest in looks and sudden change in behavior. As John cried out for help the only way he knew how: by fighting my cousin, he was kicked out and left on the streets. We, as a people, don't expect suicide to occur. This is not the first occurrence of suicide in my family. I remember the phone call in the summer of 1996 when another cousin of mine, Kevin, also committed suicide. Kevin had always had a problem with drugs. When your self-esteem reaches below a certain point, cigarettes, sex, drugs and alcohol become targets to get away from yourself, even if it is just temporary. At his eulogy, his big brother said that life was like a jacket and Kevin could never get a good fit for the jacket. It was always uncomfortable on him. The story as I overheard it in various conversations was that Kevin had come home after being out for days on a drug high, and his mother said that enough is enough; it was time for Kevin to go. He had lived on the streets before and did not want to go back so the father of five thought he was not worthy enough of living. He was not worthy enough to see another beautiful day, and with his mom in the very next room, he killed himself.

Your self-esteem determines everything in life. As I talked to my cousin, he still asks what happened? As I look at the situation I have with my children's father, I too ask what happened? How do we go from being head over heels in love and building a family with three children, to not even speaking? It is self-esteem. As the secret reveals, you attract what you are and when we met years ago, we were attracted through commonality. Over the years, I wanted to continue to grow and my children's father did not. Change is a healthy part of life. It might be said that life is 10%

what happens and 90% your reaction to it. Failure is the learning curve of Entrepreneurship, and to me the only failure is quitting, and WINNERS NEVER QUIT. I have seen my own business go through many ups and downs in our short years, but flexibility has been the key to small businesses seizing the opportunity in a downturn market. It is the downturn that allows the entrepreneurs with vision to make the changes necessary to survive and thrive in this economy.

I know what happened to our relationship now: he does not think he is worthy of me (tru dat!). I know that and he knows that, but to his children he will always be the man. Unfortunately, he does not think he is worthy of filling those shoes because of my success. We still have each other's cell numbers, and my children still call, but he is too afraid to answer the phone. America has found an interesting way to separate the black family without even trying. It used to be the bosses job to berate the man so he could come home and take his anger out on the woman, but now Corporate America just hires the woman in a white collar job and she can come home to the blue collar man and berate him for not earning enough income to take care of the family. His other alternative is letting his ego dictate that he leave the woman with the white collar job to be with a woman who makes less money than him. That is the reason there are many so called successful minority (not just black) women still single. My definition of success is not related to wealth. My definition of success is answering those two questions: Who Am I and what am I here for?

Most people meet me and say I am the happiest person they know and I believe them. Because I know who I am and what I am here for. I live everyday (including this moment at 12:11 am on Saturday night to write this book) knowing who I am and what I am here for. I called my cousin last Sunday to find out when the funeral would be, and he told me Thursday. Thursday was the one day of the week I could not go. Thursday, the Newman Networks[14] networking event would take place in the morning, Thursday was the deadline for an important 'Request for Proposal' and Thursday evening I would be recognized for Networker of the Year. Though my cousin did not understand, I would not be able to attend. A good friend said to me, "family comes first" and she said she would be there. I agree that family does come first, and Philadelphia is my family. But before we can change the world, we have to start at home. Thursday, there was a funeral with over 1,000 people in Bloomfield, Connecticut, crying over the loss of another young man, while I had the honor and privilege of sharing my story to over 300 attendees at the African American Museum to inspire them and let them know that we can make economic opportunity by working as a collective and networking together. Yes, family does come first! See, my role on Thursday was to use his death to strengthen my resolve as entrepreneurship being a solution to many problems we face as a community and educating others about the mental health disease of despair. Entrepreneurship requires that you answer the two basic questions of life: who am I and what am I here for?

There was a time when I was fifteen that I thought about killing myself. I too had thought I was not worthy of the space my body took here on this earth (teenagers are crazy!) As I stood in the kitchen with the butcher knife (ironic don't you think since, it was a butcher knife that I got stabbed with a year later?). I cried out under my breath for help. It was as of I heard a voice telling me that there were plans for my life, so I kindly put the knife back in the holder (I must not have learned much because I still have knives in my kitchen now).

That was the day I became free. I no longer cared about what people thought about Nicole Newman. I learned to become true to myself and my path. There were a lot of behaviors that took me years to comprehend, but now I am at the point where I accept them as being a part of me. The growth of my business is 100% dependent on the growth of me. I myself cannot grow unless I understand myself. Answering the question "Who am I?", Also known as your 'Unique Value Proposition' is something one may ask after knowing the reason for his/her existence.

Part of your benefit to the world, is to spread your unique value among as many as possible and contribute to their success! Another question, after why do you exist, and who are you, is 'how do you get paid for being YOU?' It took my business four different business models to get to the point where I get paid to be me. I am able to take the 72,000 I paid for my MBA, and come up with a website that allows a business to get all my knowledge and wisdom for just 15.00 a month. That is how I am able to spread my Unique Value Proposition among as many people as possible. What I learned through the different business models is that most people equate value with cost. How could I offer so much in value for so little in cost? I wanted to bring Deloitte Consulting skills valued at 300 per hour to small business owners, and I used technology solutions to lower the cost from 300 per hour to 25 per month. If business owners don't take advantage that, it's there loss and not mine, because I know who I am and what I am here for.

John, even though I was not there, my heart remembers for you. Your life inspires me to help as many people as I can answer these two questions of life - who am I and what am I here for.

"Failure dies at the feet of decision.
Decide that you want change more
than you are afraid of it."

Sulaiman Rahman 2012,
Organo Gold Blue Diamond
My Mentor,

NICOLE NEWMAN

www.nicole-newman.com

Chapter 12: My Mentor

Today as I was debating about what I would write about, Allah, in his infinite wisdom, gave me the answer. One of my mentee's (I did not even consider her a mentee) said she felt so lucky to be 22 years old and have a wealth of knowedge at her fingertips (and in her favorite new toy, the iPhone.) I just looked at her and said, "Isn't it supposed to be this way?" She said, "Yes it is", however, usually she does not see it happen. I said, "It happened for you because firstly, you made yourself available so it could happen, and secondly, we (the mentors) see value in you." We mentor people who are coachable and we can see as a success story in the making I also said to her, "I have been fortunate to have million-dollar businesses in my phone who take the time to mentor me so I could take the time to mentor you." That is the definition of lifting as we climb.

When I met Curtis Jones Jr. at the MPR Summit (Rainmakers where is number 2?) and shared my story about Newman Networks[15], he said I was well on my way, but now that I have a mentor (I actually have quite a few), to go back and find a mentee. What he said that day struck a nerve in my foundation. He said, "It is up to us to save us." And we do that through being good stewards of his blessing and sharing our knowledge by mentoring.

This was my Commentary for the Newman Networks[16] Newsletter from August 2007:

Just the other day, I sat with a coach who is also one of the business owners on the Newman Networks[17] website. We were talking about ways to improve and market the website. She said that when she sent out an e-mail to her distribution list telling her she can be found on Newman Networks[18], some of responses came back telling her that she was too professional to be associated with the businesses on the website. I started rubbing my eyebrows in frustration and I kindly said, "It's that exact attitude that got us here in the first place!" Those businesses that you think are not professional enough need your exact skills to be successful. By saying your business is too good to be listed with other businesses on this website, then you are turning your back on yourself. I say this because your business is judged by how people view the good and bad habits of people who have the same color of your skin.

When I worked at Deloitte, I was one of the first black people in my department. I knew if I did a bad job, another black person would be denied yet another opportunity. My track record when I left allowed Deloitte to judge my successor by the content of his resume not the color of his skin. My successor in fact was a black person. We have to stop pretending that these children committing crime and those businesses who don't have a certain ook are not "our" people. The sooner we realize that we are all in this together, the more successful we will all be. By being listed on this website, you expose your business to the businesses in your category and they can see how good the competition is and what it takes to measure up. Just by listing your business, you are MENTORING.

As a student of color in graduate school, the school assigned me a mentor so I could successfully complete the program. My mentor, Gina Frizzell, helped me navigate the campus and my move to the Washington D.C. area. She not only told me how to do the right thing but also what I was coing wrong. For example, I am a double dipper. That is when you dip the chip, take a bite and dip the chip again. She told me that it is an easy way to spread germs, and I need to order my own separate dip. With those few words, I continue to be a double dipper, but now I do not spread germs. My mentor and I both successfully completed graduate school, and now, ten years later, we remain close friends.

It is not fair to criticize people when you have not empowered them with your knowledge. We have to learn that there is a formula to success and current business owners are missing an opportunity to teach the next generation of business owners how to navigate the roadblocks that come with starting a business. I get the feeling that it is selfish thinking, i.e., if I can make it on my own, why should I help someone else?

Fortunately for me, I count my blessings every day. As a mom of three young children, I am well aware that I cannot survive alone. My next door neighbors and friends put it on their shoulders to help a sister out. Will, Sulaiman and Malik G., I cannot thank you enough for being "real" men and making sure the family is taken care of. My community (teachers, family, neighbors, friends, parents of friends) sent me to the best schools in the city and gave me the confidence to go to college and beyond. I remember one of my BFF's took me downtown to shop for my first year in college at the University of North Carolina at Greensboro, where she spent 200 dollars of her own money and she was in the 11th grade!

Mentoring does not just happen in business. Mentoring happens all the time. My BFF's mom said to me before I went off to college, "It coes not pay to get a C." Understanding that I was paying for the grades I got in school led me to only get two C's in both college and graduate school and I still have a 50,000 college bill!. My job as a parent is to mentor my children into productive members of society and because of my family history my approach is through entrepreneurship. Yes, at age 18 they will be adults, but will they have the skills to fly the coop and survive in the jungle of adulthood? Will they be morally grounded so the decisions and actions will be determined by their integrity and understanding the consequences of their decisions?

I cannot talk about mentoring without giving props to my mom who made sure I was placed in an environment of success. Success will not be achieved by working alone. Success comes in groups. As I look at all the success stories from relationships my life, quite a few happened from the success factory of Masterman School. I have a 50,000 grad school bill, because University of Maryland charged for being able to break bread with future presidents of fortune 500 companies, not for the education in the classrooms. It is the environment of creating relationships and sharing information that breeds success. My mom shared a secret with me that I have the pleasure of sharing with you. All decisions/rule/codes are made by people. There is a person who builds the rule and there is a person who enforces it. Nine times out of ten, the decision maker is not the boss. It is his/her secretary. They are the gatekeepers to the ears and signature pads for the decision maker. That is why I am adamant about the internet and networking. Networking environments allow me to bypass the gatekeepers and get directly on the decision makers calendar. Furthermore, because information on my company is readily available, the decision maker does not have to ask anyone about Nicole Newman. By using networking and the internet, we have been able to win 70% of the decision, the meeting is just confirmation of the capabilities.

There is no such thing as a self-made millionaire. My mentor, Sulaiman, please excuse me for messing this story up in advance, shared this network marketing story with me. A father asked his son to push a heavy cart filled with bags of sand up a hill. The son was trying and trying and he said, "Dad, I can't". The father replied back, "Use all your strength," and the son said, "I am, but it won't budge!" After trying and trying, the son finally gave up. The father said, "I asked you to use all your strength." the son replied, "I did." The father then said, "No, you didn't, because you never asked me to help." We are letting our community drown by not using our collective strength to build a tight network of independence that comes when we control the economic conditions. The economic condition we face is controlled by our ability to work collectively, and our ability to communicate or withhold information. It is mentoring environments (like a network) that make it happen. Synergy will not be generated by two individuals, but it will be when a group of people are moving together. How slave masters controlled the flock was by cutting off the information needed to communicate (e.g. reading).

Growing up, I found it very difficult to accept NO. I understood that no meant 'not now', and there will be a future opportunity for YES. My four year old son knows this and uses his charm to get the YES later. Just the other day, I told him to stay downstairs, he sat for a minute then he asked me could he go up stairs to find his truck. I said YES and when I looked around 30 minutes later he was still upstairs. Even in his still developing mind, NO is not concrete. Business owners must take the same approach to get past the hurdles that will surely come in starting your business. It is through reading books to develop your knowledge base, being in a positive environment and listening to your instinct that allows the right relationships and people to come into your life for a mentor relationship or open up your schedule to a mentee relationship. Both are needed to stop the ship from drowning and let the information flow and lift as we climb.

Love is not about "It's your fault", but "I'm sorry". Not "Where are you?", but "I'm right here". Not "How could you?", but "I understand". Not "I wish you were", but "I'm thankful you are".

Chapter 13: My Gift of Love

Network marketing has been a blessing in my life. As most minorities know access to capital is a barrier we have yet to overcome when it comes to financing our businesses. Network Marketing and my real estate investments allow a person to self-finance their business. To get the capital required, I had done what most business owners do and leveraged my assets. A traditional brick and mortar business costs hundreds of thousands of dollars to start, and I took a 20,000 line of credit against my house and utilized all my personal credit. I was pretty close to having to let go of my dream, when my mentor, Sulaiman Rahman, came along to teach me how to use the income generated in through a network marketing business to self-finance my traditional business. Traditional businesses take 3-5 years to get in profit mode and network marketing businesses can get into profit mode within a manner of days. So we can use the profit from the network marketing business to use as capital for the traditional business. He also showed me a system that teaches people how to grow their business through becoming a better person. Sulaiman could show me these things because I knew he had used the same system for his business. I did not want to hear it from a college professor who never owned a business, I needed to learn from someone who had walked in my shoes and could show me the way.

A few years ago, I had the pleasure of attending our national network marketing convention and hearing from the keynote speaker, Stedman Graham, adjunct professor and NY Times best-selling author. He shared his personal story and spoke about the most powerful feeling in the world: LOVE. Being in LOVE can make a woman go crazy but being in LOVE can also be the source of your power. It is the LOVE of what you do that makes passion, and as Steve Sanders shared with me, money follows passion. As Stedman explained, whether you are rich or poor, we are all given 24 hours in a day. The trick to life is spending most of your 24 hours doing the things you LOVE, or in my case, associating myself with the people I LOVE. I am the happiest person I know because GOD buildd a path for me to LOVE what I do and granted me the knowledge to obey H m at the same time. I have the privilege of serving his will 24 hours a day, seven days a week. These are the things that I LOVE:

1. Meeting new business owners.

2. Building relationships with my clients.

3. Teaching my clients how to use technology to make their businesses better.

4. Creating a journal of the experience.

I did not even add the most important LOVE to the list, but Stedman found a great way to say it on his website: "There are no limits to what you can accomplish when you know who you are." The requirement to having a life of abundance is to be dedicated and have ambition!

I grew up an only child with a broken heart, and like most children think, I thought I was different than everybody else. What I have learned is that we are all different. Societal pressures from peers, TV and parents, do injustice by telling children they have to fit in. As anyone has seen me interact with my own children, I encourage them to be who they are. This was a lesson I learned from my mom. She always encouraged me to not live by someone else's standards, but be true to myself. My mother did not say this in words, she showed it in her actions. My mom has five living sisters and three brothers, but she is black to their white. Though her whole family resides in Washington D.C., she chose to raise me in Philadelphia. When I was a little girl, we would go to the University of Penn's theatre to watch children's movies and we would be the only people there. Our favorite show was the classic BBC series of Dr. Who starring Tom Baker. It is a sci-fi drama about a man who travels in time using a telephone booth. Tom Baker is actually the 4th Dr. Who (and the best), staring in the series from 1974 – 1981. Yes, my mom did not conform to anybody's rules, and she passed a lot of that posture to me, but during my teenage years, raging hormones got the best of me. During that time, I stopped liking myself and lost value in the uniqueness of me. At the age of 15, I was trying so hard to be like everyone else so I could "fit in". At the same age, I was also trying to accept the privileges and responsibilities that are incurred with the transition into adulthood.

Fast forward to March 2006, when my first network marketing company, Quixtar, said the words that a 250 pound mother of a four year old, two year old and a one year old needed to hear. "Wealth is not made, it is attracted. You attract what you are, so to attract more, you must become more." My sponsor's mentor then went on to say, "One of a determining factor in a woman's income is her weight. Being overweight is not attractive, so you must change it to attract more." Now everyone will say, Oprah did not lose weight but if you read her story, when she started out in broadcasting she was a size 6. Even so she is the exception; if you look at the media commercials there is pressure to be thin. What I realize can be summed in this quote: "The world sees you how you see yourself." People are attracted to positive, happy people, and as a group, business owners and people who exercise are generally happy people. Business owners are happy because they are doing what they LOVE, and people who exercise are happy because, it is said, the happiness endorphin is released by the brain with aerobic exercise. Using these two forces is powerful for attracting wealth, because The Secret tells us that we attract what we are. Now, we can attract like-minded happy people who are also business owners (simple isn't it!). Now that I know the formula to attraction marketing, I can do what GOD designed me to do when he gave me a broken heart from my dad and a desire to find knowledge of self from my mom.

My job is to encourage you as a person, by loving the thing that you set in your heart to develop, which is YOUR Business! You were the person that birthed the idea into a vision and labored it into existence. You were the person who broke from the norm and became a 'five percenter'. They say 5% because just 5% of the U.S. population own businesses. Now, we get to come along and be a part of your marketing team and LOVE your business as much as you do, and teach you the tips and tricks learned in MBA school, and as a Deloitte consultant, to make your business better! Newman Networks utilized our technology skills to build Newman-Network.com[19], which enhances our capacity to serve as many clients as possible in our 24 hours, unlike a traditional business consultant who can only serve but a few during their 24 hours. By using this system, we lowered the cost tremendously from $300 per hour to $25 per month. In the downturn economy with big businesses falling by the wayside, small businesses are playing in the ballpark with home–field advantage!

What took me almost 20 years to figure out is that becoming a better person means LOVING the things I do well, and UNDERSTANDING but not changing the things I don't. I thought becoming a better person meant changing the fundamental value system of Nicole Newman. I tried with no luck to change my value system, because I have what other people would call character flaws. While I have a desire to help others, willingness to learn and a work-ethic that is strong - I don't like cook, clean, or do homework. I also have a tendency to be a little out-spoken. What I realize now is that becoming a better person means understanding and LOVING me, warts and all!. How I deal with the warts is to find ways to eliminate them. We can hire chefs, cleaning ladies and tutors. Those jobs are important, but I serve everyone better by concentrating on the people and things that I love. We are not meant to be perfect, but we are meant to make harmony and synergy by attracting other people who accept you the way you are and you accept them the way they are.

Businesses are built with people. Network Marketing taught me that you have to find at least five individuals who can work together to build synergy.

144

Greatness will be achieved when the whole is greater than the sum of the individual parts! Fran Tarkenton said "TEAMS win, INDIVIDUALS don't". Newman Networks was started April 2006, and it took me almost three years to find five individuals who will put their egos aside to make the whole greater than the individual units. We are developing a traditional business that will operate a network marketing business and use the LOVE of our respective crafts (marketing, service, accounting, information technology, human resources, law etc.) to attract wealth and show others how to attract wealth using the awesome power of LOVE! That, my friends, is my gift and the source of my passion. We make sure your business is not part of the 50% of all business that fail within the first three years by providing marketing tools that your business can afford. LOVE is one of the most powerful words and forces in the universe, and it was said, "There are no limits to what you can accomplish when you know who you are."

References:

1. DiversePhilly.com was taken down in 2010 and the new site is Newman-Network.com

2. www.womensbusinessresearch.org/facts/index.php

3. DiversePhilly.com was taken down in 2010 and the new site is Newman-Network.com

4. DiversePhilly.com was taken down in 2010 and the new site is Newman-Network.com

5. www.educatedsista.org

6. www.pacyber.org, www.pavcs.org and www.palcs.org

7. www.babyzone.com/kids/discipline/positive-parenting-power_73633

8. DiversePhilly.com was taken down in 2010 and the new site is Newman-Network.com

9. DiversePhilly.com was taken down in 2010 and the new site is Newman-Network.com

10. DiversePhilly.com was taken down in 2010 and the new site is Newman-Network.com

11. www.mshale.com/2008/10/02/black-unemployment-grows-past-11-percent/

12. DiversePhilly.com was taken down in 2010 and the new site is Newman-Network.com

13. http://www.uphs.upenn.edu/ficap/forum/docs/feb03joe. pdf

14. DiversePhilly.com was taken down in 2010 and the new site is Newman-Network.com

15. DiversePhilly.com was taken down in 2010 and the new site is Newman-Network.com

16. DiversePhilly.com was taken down in 2010 and the new site is Newman-Network.com

17. DiversePhilly.com was taken down in 2010 and the new site is Newman-Network.com

18. DiversePhilly.com was taken down in 2010 and the new site is Newman-Network.com

19. DiversePhilly.com was taken down in 2010 and the new site is Newman-Network.com

Educated Sista's was used by permission of the Educated Sistas' Association[5]. Educated Sistas' Association is a public charitable non-profit 501(c)(3), tax exempt organization committed to lifelong learning with a dedicated staff and volunteers providing FREE adult-literacy, GED preparation, and workforce training to name a few.

Acknowledgements

I have so many to thank for coming this far and believing that we can go further starting with Allah ta'ala and his Prophet Muhammad sallallahu ^alayi wa sallam.

Family: My mom Gwen Newman and her brothers and sisters, my dad Warren Newman and his family, my children's father, my children and tutors - Sahar, Omar and Nasir, my BFF's who have been uplifting me for so long (28 years and still going strong) - Tiffany Mosley-Adeyemo, The Suluki Family, Myesha Brown-Davis , Kafi Hakim, Bronwyn Scott, my mentor who not only showed me the path but took my hand and led me ALL the way Sulaiman Rahman, Andrew who knew it was his duty to give me the Shahadah, Tanisha, Rashan, Gigi (my grandmother) who shined her light on me, my cousins Russell Bradshaw and Donnell Payne who were more like brothers and allowed us to grow up as friends.

Business: My accountability partner who brings wisdom daily Tara Colquitt, my first team member who watch it happen Samira Robinson (so proud of you Dust Bunny!), Lisa Jeter, Colin Williams , Aginah

Carter-Shabazz who said go for it and brought me to the artist Hasan Shaheed, Rochelle Davis who allowed me to have my first big event at Girlfriends and introduced me to the team of Whitney Thomas and Meredith Marshall-Sabir and last but certainly not least, my partners Greg Graphics and Why PR and Marketing.

My second family: - Sister Hidaya, Sister Rayan, Sister Khayriyyah, Sister Michaela, Abd, Brother Bashir, Brother Imad, Hajj Ali, Shakyh Ra'id, Sister Muklisah, Hajjah Aisha, and my neighbor who instantly became my sister girlfriend Sister Hadayah.

www.ingramcontent.com/pod-product-compliance
Lightning Source LLC
Chambersburg PA
CBHW021006090426
42738CB00007B/672